BEAUTIFUL LOFTY PEOPLE

Other books by Helen Bevington

Doctor Johnson's Waterfall (1946)

Nineteen Million Elephants (1950)

A Change of Sky (1956)

When Found, Make a Verse Of (1961)

Charley Smith's Girl (1965)

A Book and a Love Affair (1968)

The House Was Quiet and the World Was Calm (1971)

Beautiful Lofty People

Helen Bevington

HARCOURT BRACE JOVANOVICH, INC.
NEW YORK

N.C.
814
B

Printed in the United States of America

Some of the poems and essays in this volume originally appeared in *The
American Scholar, The Archive, The New York Times Book Review,* and
Southern Poetry Review. "The Man Montaigne," "The Lady of the Château,"
"Advice (a Little) Useful" appeared in the author's book *A Change of Sky*
(Houghton Mifflin, 1956); "I Would Be John Chester," "Oliver's Warts,"
"Emily to Her Niece," "Aunt Mary Emerson and the Worm," "Mrs.
Trollope in America" in her *Dr. Johnson's Waterfall* (Houghton Mifflin,
1946); "Of Dorothy Wordsworth," "The Suitor of Christina Rossetti" (as
"Mr. Cayley"), "Mr. White Walking" (as "Mr. White of Selborne") in
her *Nineteen Million Elephants* (Houghton Mifflin, 1950); "Cassandra and
Jane" in her *When Found, Make a Verse Of,* copyright 1961 by Helen
Bevington, reprinted by permission of Simon & Schuster. "John Bois, Note-
taker" appeared in *The New York Times Book Review* (as "Translating
for King James"), copyright © 1970 by The New York Times Company,
reprinted by permission.

Library of Congress Cataloging in Publication Data

Bevington, Helen (Smith), date
   Beautiful lofty people.

   Essays.
   1. Literature—Addresses, essays, lectures.
I. Title.
PN37.B45   809   73-17082
ISBN 0-15-111310-6

First edition

B C D E

FOR PEGGY

"It is no use trying to sum people up.
One must follow hints, not exactly what
is said, nor yet entirely what is done."
—VIRGINIA WOOLF, *Jacob's Room*

Contents

BEAUTIFUL LOFTY PEOPLE

Beautiful Lofty People

They were lofty in their search for something, or in their
singular view of life, never toplofty. Montaigne sought for
serenity in himself, Sir Thomas More for *festivitas,* Colette
for a way of looking. Eliot sought for Little Gidding, the
way to peace; Yeats for Byzantium, the holy city of his
imagination. Often, like Rabelais and Sydney Smith, they
were merry men; they laughed at the performance.

Yeats in his poem "Beautiful Lofty Things" lists the
people he loved in the way he remembered them—in beautiful lofty moments. There was his great friend John
O'Leary, the Fenian leader. There was Yeats's father,
climbing to the stage of the Abbey Theatre to quiet a rag-
ing mob. Drunken Standish O'Grady, addressing a drunken
audience in "high nonsensical words." Lady Gregory at
Coole during the Irish troubles, defying a threat to her life.
Maud Gonne, a Pallas Athene, standing at the Howth
station in Dublin—each revealing himself in look and act
and gesture,

All the Olympians; a thing never known again.

The idea of the men and women one loves for their own
sake caught in a lofty moment, intense with life, may help
to explain the inclusion here of a slut and a drunkard like
Bet Flint. And no harm done.

The *Festivitas* of Sir Thomas More

The word for him is *festivitas*. Yet his life, had someone else lived it, would seem calamitous, unbearably tragic.

He lived for fifty-seven years and then was put to death. Through his refusal to support Henry VIII in his claim to be Supreme Head of the Church of England or to sign the Oath of Supremacy which went, More said, against his conscience and would imperil his soul, More was found guilty of high treason and beheaded at the Tower of London, July 5, 1535. Afterward his head was exposed on London Bridge till his daughter Margaret took it down and carried it home to preserve in spices till she died. Perhaps it was buried with her. He was a peaceable and loving man, a just and equable man, but for putting God before his king, Henry had him murdered.

Only Margaret knew of his punishing his body with whips to subdue it, the cords knotted to tame his flesh till the blood came. It was she who washed the hair shirt he wore next to his skin. In his youth More had longed for the monastic life and for four years lived with the monks of Charterhouse in London, tempted to take the final vows. He longed for that peace. Instead he returned to the world, went courting at the house of John Colt who had three daughters, and, though most attracted to the middle girl, married the eldest, Jane, lest she be hurt if rejected for her sister. Jane became the "little wife" he so faithfully loved, the mother of his children, Margaret, Elizabeth, Cecily, and a son John. Then Jane Colt died. More's second wife, Mistress Alice Middleton, was a widow and a scold, a dull-hearted woman older than he with whom he lived content, often adjuring her to be merry.

4

Merry. The word stayed ever on More's tongue and in his heart. To Dame Alice he said, "I pray you with my children be merry in God." From the Tower during the last fifteen months of his life, he wrote to Margaret, "I beseech Him make you all merry in the hope of Heaven." The day before his execution he sent her the hair shirt and a letter written with a piece of coal: "Tomorrow I long to go to God; it were a day very meet and convenient for me."

On the morrow as he climbed the scaffold, which was weak and ready to fall, More said, "I pray you, Master Lieutenant, see me safe up, and for my coming down let me shift for myself." By light words he took his leave. Without solemnity, with courtesy and compassion for others, with a cheerful serene face and three jests on the scaffold he went to die, speaking to the executioner, "Pluck up thy spirits, man, and be not afraid to do thine office. My neck is very short." He removed his beard from the block, "for it at least hath not offended the king."

The test of a man in the *Utopia* is the way he dies. Those who die "merrily and full of good hope, for them no man mourneth." They are praised for their merry death and monuments are erected to them. More showed how it was done. He died as he had lived.

William Roper, More's son-in-law and husband to Margaret, attempted to measure his shining worth. In the sixteen years of living in More's genial house and being daily conversant with him, said Roper, "I could never perceive him as much as once in a fume."

He was never angry. His character was marked by kindness. As described by Erasmus (who loved that tranquillity he himself couldn't find and loved More, who had enough for both), he was of medium height, fair complexion, auburn hair, thin beard, blue-gray eyes, his face alight forever breaking into a smile, merry of word and manner.

Quarrels were unknown in his hospitable house. He loved gaiety and wit (but not at another's expense), and in fits of laughter ruled his household. His gift for friendship was immense. He had an easiness that made him forget even the gravest injuries.

John Aubrey in *Brief Lives* calls More "extraordinary facetious." One night when More was riding with friends, suddenly he crossed himself and cried out, "Jesu Maria! doe not you see that prodigious Dragon in the skye?" They all looked but nobody could see it. Then one did spy it, and the rest promptly saw it too. Everybody saw it. "Whereas there was no such phantome," says Aubrey. He tells of a time when Roper came to More's house with a proposal to marry one of his daughters. More led the young man into the bedchamber where, since it was morning, two of them lay still asleep. Taking the sheet by the corner and whipping it off, More revealed the girls lying on their backs, their smocks up to their armpits. Thus awakened, they stirred and turned on their bellies. "Quoth Roper, 'I have seen both sides,' and so gave a patt on the buttock he made choice of, sayeing, 'Thou art mine.' " You can still hear the laughter at that wooing.

More's favorite jest, told him by his father, he would repeat to tease the females in his house: "A good Woman (as the old Philosopher observeth) is but like one Ele put in a bagge amongst 500 Snakes, and if a man should have the luck to grope out that one Ele from all the snakes, yet he hath at best a wet Ele by the Taile."

In a letter to his children More wrote, "If ever I flogged you, it was but with a peacock's tail." By giving them the greatest praise in the world, which is approval, he taught them and made them love learning—the son and the three daughters, who studied with their father Greek and Latin, logic, philosophy, theology, astronomy. (They learned the Greek alphabet by shooting bows and arrows at the letters.) As one would expect, he believed in the equality of the sexes. "Both are reasonable beings," he said, "suited equally for those studies by which reason is cultivated."

Incredulous and amazed, Erasmus viewed More's happy family life that grew to contain some twenty members: "There is not any man living so affectionate to his children as he, and he loveth his old wife as if she were a girl of fifteen." In this commodious house in Chelsea, Holbein is said to have stayed three years. Erasmus, a difficult guest who spoke no English, loathed the smell of fish and the taste of English beer, wrote *The Praise of Folly* while laid up with lumbago and dedicated it to his beloved friend: "I chose to amuse myself with a praise of folly (*moria*) because of your name of More, which comes as close to the word for folly as you are far from the thing itself." Erasmus said, "We had but one soul between us." His praise of More became a litany.

Besides this huge family, More kept a noisy collection of birds and animals inside the house and in the garden— a monkey, rabbits, a fox, a ferret, a weasel. On all of life he lavished love; he found joy in everything; his *festivitas* never forsook him. And since his fate was to die a martyr and be made a saint, thank God he was a merry one.

Montaigne's "Scandalous Serenity"

How did Montaigne achieve serenity? In his biography of the man, Donald Frame writes: "What draws us to Montaigne is not something we share but something we lack: the scandalous serenity of his self-acceptance." I do nothing, said Montaigne, without blitheness.

Few of us are able to say that.

The most tragic loss in his life was of his one perfect friend, La Boétie, whose early death he never ceased to mourn with a grief so heavy that for a time Montaigne considered suicide. He lost all but one of his children. He had no son. As the years passed, Montaigne failed to remember how many children it was he had had and lost, "two or three" he said, who died in childhood. Actually he had six daughters, of whom only Léonor lived.

Three females made up his household, though it seems clear women played an insignificant part in that serenity. In his essay "Of Vanity," Montaigne confessed he did not have, as his father had had, a passionate love for his household. It is myself that I portray, he wrote, omitting mention of such secondary characters as mother, wife, and child. Of his mother, who survived him, he tells nothing. His marriage was humdrum. To his wife Françoise he was a dutiful but indifferent husband. While he tried to avoid domestic crises as occasions for vexation, he never contrived well enough: the pinpricks were tiny, soon forgotten but pinpricks. He was not one to omit mention of them, "the throng of petty troubles."

Of his only child (unfortunately female with "the ordinary weakness of the sex") he said, "I do not involve myself at all in directing her." A daughter must be brought up by women; her most useful and honorable occupation was to be a neat housewife. Had he any sons, he would wish them his own good fortune, "the good father that God gave me," though as a father himself Montaigne saw no irony in that remark. He would be glad in old age for a son-in-law to manage his affairs. "But we live in a world where loyalty in our own children is unknown." It was better therefore to have no express need of anyone. King Lear learned the same lesson.

Montaigne lived in cruel and terrible times. "I have gone to bed a thousand times in my own home, imagining that someone would betray me and slaughter me that very night." Yet in the midst of danger he thought not so much how to escape as how little it mattered that he escape. Unafraid in an age of terror—of eight civil wars and the bloody massacre of the Huguenots—in a menacing world so much like our world, he wrote, "Anyone who is only sacrilegious and a parricide in our days is a good and honorable man."

During his fifty-nine years, he suffered intense physical pain from the stone, bore it, and stayed serene—scandalously so. No man could call him insensitive. The way to meet life, he thought, was on its own terms. Death happens only once, it happens to all: "What of it? We are all wind." He accepted the role nature had dealt him; reality satisfied him. He measured his coat according to his cloth.

It sounds hard to do. It was. The answer long sought and slowly reached was self-acceptance. Finding himself without any other wealth, Montaigne presented himself to himself. It became a lifelong encounter, to observe, take stock, taste, "roll about" in himself, to cultivate his authenticity, to find a soul he could call his own.

In Montaigne's view one man's life is everyman's, which justified taking its measure. So long as there were ink and paper in the world, he would make a record of his life, blazon his actions. That they were humble and inglorious mattered not at all. "And if no one reads me, have I wasted my time entertaining myself?" He happened not to enjoy the amusements available to him, such as building houses, hunting, gardening, other country pleasures. He didn't know good wines or foods, how to train a bird, how to treat a sick horse or dog. He cared nothing for music or games. Nor did a public life interest him. The most stupid study (to one who always mislaid his purse) was to weigh his money and count it over. What he really liked to do was what he did: "My art and métier is to live."

And since Montaigne chose to make his great study of *moi-même*, about whom he was the most learned man alive, we are free to make a study of Montaigne, that is, if we wish to learn about ourselves. It is a subject, he said, that would interest neither scholars nor fools.

When Emerson read the *Essays*, he believed they were written expressly for him. In gratitude he said, "It seemed to me as if I myself had written the book in some former life, so sincerely it spoke to my thoughts and experience." Brave Emerson! Had he ever for a moment possessed Montaigne's vigorous lusts? Of his own sex life, would he have confessed to the reader that he couldn't make love standing up, or have written, "I shall never be grateful to impotence for any good it may do me"? Would you find him discussing the regularity of his bowels? When I read Emerson, he speaks neither to me nor about me, because I'm not like him. Yet we are both like Montaigne, who belongs to us all. Or perhaps he helps me to belong to myself.

From his tower, to which he retired at thirty-eight, Montaigne could look down on his house, garden, courtyard. Up there he was strictly alone and easy. Twenty years of solitude (except for a brief period as mayor of Bordeaux) were his for the taking, "without wife, without children, without possessions, without retinue and servants, so that, when the time comes to lose them, it will be nothing new to do without them." Above the five rows of shelves containing the thousand books that lined his circular library and curved around him, he placed a number of mottoes to live by: "I am a man; nothing human is alien to me." Another was: "*Que sçais-je?*"

"What do I know?" He knew himself. He knew his own ignorance. "I would hardly dare tell of the vanity and weakness I find in myself." Yet he did tell. And of that ignorance Montaigne knew better than to repent, aware though he was of speaking it pompously and opulently, of speaking knowledge meagerly and piteously. One must be content to be arbitrary, he said (quoting Socrates, *According to one's power*), since there are many views of truth and many experiences. One may say of life only this much: "I will see it this way."

Detachment was a necessary part: to be serene one learns to be detached. The aim of life was happiness, and the happiness was in living. To laugh was better than to weep—to laugh at the fact one was laughing. Willing it so, he became a wise and happy man, whose "real profession, his only trade," said Sainte-Beuve, "was to be a human being."

Wonderful Montaigne.

Mt. Olympus touched heaven at the top. Mt. Parnassus

was the lofty abode of Apollo. Mt. Sinai a dwelling-place
of the god of the Hebrews. And Montaigne?

> They called Parnassus the hill of poetry,
> Olympus the hill of the gods,
> Sinai the hill of the law,
>
> The three eternal holy mountains
> Sacred to the gods,
> And the gods are dead.
>
> What would you call him,
> Michel de Montaigne—
> The hill of doubt? The skeptic in his tower?
>
> O, the many mountains.

The Man Montaigne

He said he was content
By nature and by design,
And I read his words
Wishing they were mine.
And I think his thoughts
Secondhandedly,
As if they had come
Of my own temerity.

Yet to be like him
Takes gaiety beside
Dispassion of the heart,
Takes being satisfied
To ask, "What do I know?"
And hear only a dim
"Nothing" for reply—
To be content like him.

Colette and the Word *Regarde*

Colette had a word, a simple imperative, to be applied to everyday, to everyone, to everything. It was Sido's word, her mother's whom she adored: "Sido's great word was 'Look.' " Look, she would say, at the hairy caterpillar, the bean sprout, the wasp, the sunset. "Look, be quick, the bud of the purple iris is opening! Be quick, or it will open before you can see it."

Colette was a lifewatcher. To look she used all her senses at once—she heard, she touched, she breathed the world in, she stared with intense care, fixedly like a cat, hypnotized.

Regarde, the last word Colette uttered before she died, was her living word for *l'amour, la vie, le monde*. With her deep blue eyes, Look! she said, at the color blue ("I know where I stand with regard to the color blue, but I have no wish to be tricked by it"), as she wrote under the blue lamp and "the blue light creeps until it reaches the blue paper." Blue had for her its own clarity and purpose.

Look at people, she would say: recognize them, accept them as they are without wanting to change them. Look at happiness: what is it? Nothing to count on. Not a visible thing, not very important after all. "Can you live? Yes, if you are not happy. There is no virtue in felicity."

Look at yourself then, watch and wait: observe what becomes you. Three things, Colette saw, were not her style—feathered hats, general ideas ("I have never had any general ideas") and earrings. To these she added tears. "I detest tears—perhaps because I have found them so very hard to conquer."

Look at flowers (one flower at a time to learn its identity): the white gardenia that after three days resembles "a white kid glove that has fallen into a stream." The tulip, a painted Easter egg, its heavy posterior sitting on its stem. The black pansy, the velvet of it!

"We will never look enough," she wailed, "never accurately enough, never passionately enough."

That being so, we miss seeing the mirror there. We see what we want to see. It was true of Colette. Like everyone else, she generalized too much from a partial view. Without hesitation she offered conflicting statements as to what can and what cannot be seen. Lacking a ready answer, she gave one anyway.

She looked at love most of all, determined to have the last word, to define its nature and its worth. Her novels harped on love, especially the anguish and defeat of love. And she said, with authority, "The heart can begin again." But Colette knew better than that: either the heart can or it cannot. "Everything that we love despoils us," she said (everything—including her beloved cats). "Things explain themselves in the long run," she said. O, Colette, what an outrageous lie! They do or they never do.

She had less than perfect vision, of course. She had only a mortal glimpse of things. Even so. By cupping her hands before her eyes, Colette saw more than most, marveling at the landscape.

"Don't wear yourself out telling lies," she reminded herself (and anyone else who tries to write words). "Only describe what you have seen."

"LOOK!" she said. "Look for a long time at what pleases you, and longer still at what pains you."

Regarde.

A Way of Looking

Regarde, said Colette. *Regarde!*
It was her scrupulous word
For perishable things
Like passion and cats, for absurd
Beginnings and endings.
Look! she said, look around
At clouds and cuckoos, *regarde*
La douleur, le bonheur,
Et l'amour, et la vie, et le monde.

John Bois, Notetaker

As I drive from my countryside to the University of a morning, I slow down to look at the bulletin board outside a small Methodist church that I pass. I hope it will give me my fortune for today, something like "The devil is dead," perhaps. This morning it said, "Do you love me?"

Well! I laughed to myself, the preacher is getting personal. Yet had the words been "Lovest thou me?" would I have understood them better? I would have understood. Only in the King James Version do they sound like the voice of God.

Of the forty-seven known translators of that noblest version of the English Bible, or of the great undertaking itself, few records remain. They were the most learned men of their golden time, Elizabethan scholars (the general editor was the famous preacher Lancelot Andrewes), alive when Shakespeare and Bacon were alive. They made lovely the language, fit and majestic in its poetry. And they are for the most part faceless and forgotten.

One of them was John Bois, who appears before our eyes through a recent discovery of his notes on the project. He alone among the whole company, it seems, took notes, which he kept to his dying day and bequeathed to his daughter Anne. After his death in 1643, they disappeared from sight to remain lost for more than three centuries. Now Professor Ward Allen of Auburn University has edited thirty-nine pages of these notes (probably but a fragment of the whole), found intact in Corpus Christi College, Oxford, where they were buried in a collection of papers belonging to William Fulman, a fellow of Corpus

17

Christi who died in 1688. They are, in fact, copied in Fulman's hand. Where Fulman got hold of them, nobody knows.

In John Bois a remarkable man emerges to stand for the rest, a visible, very human man surrounded by a silent company—those invisible scholars who, it was said at the time, sought the truth rather than their own praise.

Yet when John Bois was appointed by King James a member of the second Cambridge group and assigned to work on the Apocrypha, there was grumbling among the Cambridge scholars at the eccentric choice. Bois was only a rector of nearby Boxworth. They disdained him and repined, complaining they needed no help from a country parson. Before them lay a monumental task for men of eminence skilled in Hebrew and Greek, hardly a chore for amateurs.

The entire text of the Bible was divided among six groups of scholars organized to revise each part—two groups working at Oxford, two at Cambridge, two at Westminster. They were furnished with forty copies of the Bishops' Bible and directed to make a close revision, consulting other translations (such as Tyndale's Bible) as need arose. They had the Hebrew text of the Old Testament beside them, the Greek text of the New. No official journal of the proceedings was ever kept. John Selden, a contemporary, left behind in *Table Talk* (not published till 1689) a brief glimpse to picture them by: "One read the translation, the rest holding in their hands some Bible. . . . If they found any fault they spoke; if not, he read on."

The performance of John Bois must have astonished and humbled them. A scholar indeed! After working in both Cambridge companies (having finished his part on the Apocrypha, he took over a section of the Old Testament at the entreaty of him to whom it was assigned. "I forbear to name him," says Walker), Bois was chosen one of the final committee of twelve to make the whole harmonious: to prepare the master copy of the King James Version and deliver it to the printers at Stationers' Hall, London. It appeared in 1611, seven years in the making, a folio volume in black letter. Bois's notes refer to this last stage of the revision, to the rephrasing of particular lines and verses from Romans through Revelation, with reference by initials to several of the other translators. Everywhere they prove his consummate skill and delicate precision. They show he had an excellent ear. They illuminate his mastery of the English tongue. ("For the ear trieth words, as the mouth tasteth meat.")

What manner of man was John Bois? One hesitates to call him a saint (an overlooked, uncloistered saint), appropriate though the role may be for those who would make audible the Word. In Anthony Walker's contemporary sketch, a charming biography first published in the eighteenth century, John Bois sounds like an earlier, more learned, lovable Parson Adams. *The Life of that famous Grecian Mr. John Bois, S.T.B.*, Walker titled the portrait of his friend.

With a scholar for father, young John mastered the Bible in Hebrew at five and wrote in Hebrew by the age of six. About his gentle mother he noted in a Book of Common Prayer: "This was my mother's book; my good mother's book. Hir name was first Mirable Poolye; and then afterwards, Mirable Bois; being so called by the name of her husband, my father, William Bois." The writer of those meticulous words was born thorough.

He knew Greek well before entering, at fourteen, St. John's College, Cambridge, where he was wondered at for his learning and "counted very early summer fruit." Besides himself, only one student in the college could write Greek. Cherished therefore by his teacher, Mr. Andrew Downes (who later worked at his side as one of the translators of the King James Version), John Bois made a habit of studying in the University library from 4:00 A.M. to 8:00 P.M. without intermission. From the start he was a four o'clock scholar.

This mania for learning led him first to the study of medicine where, as a follower of Aesculapius, he managed to acquire every fascinating disease and disorder he read about. With so vivid an imagination, John Bois was safer in the church. He contracted at least one bona fide disease, smallpox, and when elected fellow of St. John's had to be carried wrapped in blankets from his sickbed to the ceremony, after which, I suppose, everybody present came down with the plague.

He entered holy orders, was ordained, and became chief lecturer in Greek at St. John's for ten happy years. At 4:00 A.M., his finest hour, he would arise and deliver an extra lecture in his chamber, not to himself but to the willing fellows who hurried in before dawn, while the number of candles lit equaled the strokes of St. John's tolling bell.

Then came romance into John Bois's life. When he was about thirty-six, the rector of Boxworth died, leaving in his will the startling request that Mr. Bois of St. John's become his successor by marrying his daughter. Never having met the girl, a Miss Holt, this goodly man paid an obedient call at the parsonage to introduce himself before accepting the living and, a few months later, marrying what came with it. Again, imagination carried him too far. If he expected a miracle this time, he was mistaken.

At least she taught him patience. After mismanaging his

household so badly he was forced to part with his "darling (I mean his library)," says Walker, in order to pay his debts; after driving him to such misery, such estrangement from her, that he considered leaving home and England forever, she won for her pains a most loving husband and father of her seven children—one who chided not or was unkind, who gladly performed any office of love "either at entreaty or unrequested."

Instead of dwelling on possible regret, John Bois went into training to endure. He fasted sometimes twice a week, prayed kneeling on bare bricks—frequent rather than long prayers—and took in boarders to make ends meet. He walked miles daily (like Fielding's Parson Adams reading as he walked), and for the rest of his life observed strictly the following rules: Always to study standing. Never to study in a window. Never to go to bed with cold feet.

Till he died at eighty-three, now prebendary of Ely Cathedral, his serene face remained unwrinkled, his head not bald, his senses keen, his body sound, his memory intact, and his teeth perfect to the grave. He was charitable to a fault. When the neighboring poor came to his door, he told them if ever he forgot they should demand money from him as a just debt. The beggar who sat at his table was fed and taught along with students and schoolboys athirst for knowledge. Humbly he gave and forgave. He condemned no man, and no man called him proud. The story is told by Walker of a small child left in his parish by some "stragling people." Since she was not an infant nor yet old enough to give testimony of her faith, Bois sought permission to baptize her. After many refusals, he persisted till he received the order and performed the baptism himself. She was by then twenty-nine years old.

Yet in his old age he meditated long on the words of 2

Samuel, xix, 35: "I am this day fourscore years old: and can I discern between good and evil?"

John Bois endears himself as saints and innocents do, those practitioners of peace and love. Above all he lives on as a tireless, brilliant scholar, worthy of the tremendous task James I required of him. During the four years spent in Cambridge till the initial labor of revising the Bible was completed, he received no recompense whatever beyond his meals at the University. There he abode all week till Saturday night when he returned on horseback the five miles to his family and the Sunday service at Boxworth—a preacher of plain sermons who prepared with infinite care and spoke with the Bible in his hands and no notes. "Lovest thou me?" The words were on his lips.

The final revision took John Bois to London for nine arduous months of daily meetings, where like the others of the committee he was paid thirty shillings a week by the Stationers' Company. And that was all. King James had other interests, such as cockfights, the royal hunt, gaming, royal routs and revels. He was greedy and grasping. The translators received nothing whatever from him, and the money paid by the Stationers' Company did not come from the Crown. Though King James is forever glorified by a book of felicity, clarity, and grace that carries his name, yet in this thankless fashion did he reward his translators for their achievement. Incredibly, that was all.

Hester Thrale and Her Notebooks

On her thirty-fifth birthday, 1776, Hester Thrale received from her husband a set of six blank notebooks handsomely bound in calf, each cover with a red label stamped in gold: "Thraliana." It was a few weeks before their thirteenth wedding anniversary.

Invited to articulate her days (a wife who couldn't hold her tongue), she began to write down anecdotes, observations, verses, scraps, trash, "in fine everything which struck me at the time." Her first observation was of the donor, her husband whom she called "my master," the rich Southwark brewer she had married against her will, "without the smallest pretensions to passion on either side." In Volume I she undertook his character or portrait, starting with his outward appearance and writing readily enough: "Mr. Thrale's person is manly, his countenance agreeable, his eyes steady, and of the deepest blue."

A fair start. Then she lifted her pen or appeared to, took a long sighing breath, and paused for inspiration, weighing her words. What did she know of this strange man? She had borne him eleven children by this time, of whom seven were dead. After thirteen years of marriage, what could she claim for their union? That he felt any attachment for his wife? He had never professed any. Here she proceeded with obvious caution: "Though little tender of her person, he is very partial to her understanding."

As a husband he was cold. His passion, except for meat and drink, seldom disturbed his tranquillity. "His servants do not much love him," she wrote, "and I am not sure that his children have much affection for him." "Mr. Thrale boasts the coldness of his heart." "He is obliging to no-body." A silent, glum, slothful man, a libertine by habit unfaithful (though she was never fond enough to be jeal-ous), a glutton with several double chins (who within five years' time had gorged himself into apoplexy and the grave)—was there really nothing she could say of him? Nothing. Nothing at all.

"Yet one *must* know something of him after so long acquaintance."

Thirty-three years later, Mrs. Thrale—now Mrs. Piozzi —came to the end of her six large notebooks. For some 1,600 pages through a garrulous life she had chattered on, scribbling her days away—sketches of her friends, jokes, gossip, "the depository of every thought as it arose"—leaving a picture of herself as an effusively vivacious but giddy, longwinded rattle, a prattler like the Wife of Bath. Now she was a lonely old woman of sixty-eight, for the second time a widow. Until the Italian singer Gabriel Piozzi wooed her in her forties, she had never been in love. ("My heart is penetrated by its passion for Piozzi.") For him she abandoned her four daughters as they rejected her. ("May I live but to make him happy, & hear him say tis *me* that make him so.")

As she sat alone, writing the final entry of "Thraliana," March 30, 1809, with nothing more left to tell, it would seem she was distracted by grief, blinded by bitter tears: ". . . all is over; and my second husband's death is the last thing recorded in my first husband's present. Cruel death!"

The Wise Reply of Mrs. Thrale

One day Miss Owen and Miss Burney asked her,
At tea, if she had never been in love—
A withering thing to ask a married lady
Mature in years, and she the mother of
A dozen children, of whom four survived
(A piece of impudence, it seems to me).
Yet Mrs. Thrale took no offense at all
But answered laughing. "With myself," she said
To those two spinsters. "And most passionately!"

The Shoes of
Dorothy Wordsworth and Fanny Burney

There is Dorothy Wordsworth's *Journal* and there is Fanny Burney's *Diary*. Fortunately the two women never met.

Dorothy Wordsworth was a tireless walker. She suffered, I think, from *la manie ambulante*. The Alfoxden journal contains the same entries, repeated over and over, a journal of ambulation: "Walked with Coleridge over the hills." "Walked through the woods." "Walked upon the hill-tops." "Walked by moonlight." "Walked I know not where."

"I can always walk over a moor with a light foot," she said of her tour of Scotland. Coleridge went along and collapsed in no time.

Nothing kept her indoors. She went in storm and wind, in piercing cold and snow, day or night, all times and weathers. She stood still to note the mist on the hills, a foxglove by the roadside. "I saw a solitary butter-flower in the wood." "The thrush sang all day."

With her brother William, a prodigious walker to whom forty miles a day made a pleasant outing, Dorothy (leaving Mrs. Wordsworth behind to do the housework) would set off before breakfast to climb mountains, linger on steep hillsides, listen to the lowing of cattle and bleating of sheep. She loved to visit old sheepfolds. She descended like a free spirit to lakes, streams, and cataracts, impatient to gaze at the next waterfall. Soaked to the skin, lost on a strange path, overtaken by night, she never grew footsore or in need of a bath. She does mention looking forward to a cup of tea.

Miss Fanny Burney walked no farther than to her carriage or the length of a fashionable drawing room (like

Millimant in *The Way of the World,* "I nauseate walking; 'tis a country diversion"). Wherever she went she simpered. When the famous Mrs. Cholmondeley deigned to speak to her, Fanny confided to her diary, "I could only simper." Between simpers she tittered—"I am eternally upon the titter." She had the vapors as a lady ought, on occasion the fidgets. She languished, expired of fatigue, gushed, fluttered in "delicious confusion," and readily took alarm. She was thrown into "tittering and ridiculous fits" by Dr. Johnson's humor. She was a twitterer as well.

Miss Burney learned to walk backwards at court in George III's presence without treading on her train. Once she got lost in St. James's Palace merely by trying to walk from the ballroom out one door into another. It was a shattering experience.

Her worst adventure occurred on February 2, 1789, one "that has occasioned me the severest personal terror I ever experienced in my life. . . . I strolled into the gardens." The stroll was undertaken at Kew Palace when she was Second Keeper of the Queen's Robes. It happened that the King, who by this time had gone violently insane, caught sight of her and gave chase, calling out "Miss Burney! Miss Burney!" She was ready to die. Heavens, how she ran! On and on she flew along the paths till one of the King's doctors commanded her to stop, since it would hurt His Majesty to run about like that. Having cornered her, the King merely kissed her cheek, made her walk by his side while he sang in a hoarse voice a few airs from Handel.

In a world of elaborate manners, ruffles and lace and artifice, Fanny's footsteps were light but elegant, her gait mincing. Dorothy had the long swift stride of a Lake Country girl, with a brown gypsy face and wild eyes, who wouldn't know a simper, titter, or twitter if she heard one.

"She did not cultivate the graces," said De Quincey. "She was the very wildest (in the sense of the most natural) person I have ever known." Her wanderings looked to friends and neighbors little short of vagrancy. Wordsworth felt called upon to defend her in a poem, "To a Young Lady who had been reproached for taking long Walks in the Country," after their aunt Mrs. Crackenthorpe had rebuked Dorothy for rambling about the countryside alone on foot. William spurred his sister on: "Dear child of Nature, let them rail!"

Fanny was a lady, a modish Londoner, pure eighteenth-century Leicester Square. She was Dr. Johnson's "little Burney," a bit of a prude, a shy creature addicted to scribbling novels. In them as in her diary, I can't find that she ever described a bird or mentioned a flower. She never walked by moonlight.

Dorothy (only nineteen years younger) was a Dove Cottage Romantic, watching her brother approvingly as he wrote the words that shook the world, the Preface to the second edition of *Lyrical Ballads:* "September 13, 1800. Saturday morning. William writing his Preface—did not walk."

In that volume he said of her, with all his love,

> . . . let the moon
> Shine on thee in thy solitary walk;
> And let the misty mountain-winds be free
> To blow against thee.

Both women kept delightful journals, revealing their enterprises. Both were five feet tall, chaste, literate, fond of drinking tea. But only imagine the difference in their shoes.

Of Dorothy Wordsworth

"She would have discovered wonders anywhere."

What in this place would please
Her? How can I tell, of the felicities,
What sky of mine would please
Her, which leaf excel?

How can I tell—
Green lizard in the sun
Or the persimmon trees—
Of the discoveries which one?

This one?
Mockingbirds in the pine,
Profundities like the wild muscadine,
Mimosa, hers or mine.

Any of these.

William Wordsworth, Walker

It was De Quincey who calculated "upon good data" how many miles Wordsworth must have walked by middle age. He came up with the astonishing figure: 180,000 miles. Furthermore, De Quincey concluded that, by walking instead of using alcohol or other stimulants, Wordsworth lived a life of "unclouded happiness." I find the second claim even more extravagant than the first.

He was said to walk like a cade (a lamb or foal left by its mother and fed by hand)—a kind of locomotion not easy to visualize unless one knows how an abandoned lamb walks. Hazlitt tried to describe Wordsworth's walk: "There was something of a roll, a lounge in his gait, not unlike his own Peter Bell," who in the poem

> ... had a dark and sidelong walk,
> And long and slouching was his gait.

De Quincey remembered his walk as giving the impression of absolute meanness, especially when viewed from behind. Once Dorothy, catching a rear view of him, was mortified: "Is it possible—can that be William? How very mean he looks!" Though De Quincey had met Wordsworth in 1807 and was writing twenty-seven years later, the picture he drew in so sharp an outline angered the poet by its impertinence, upset his self-esteem, and put an end to his friendship with this "pest in society, and one of the most worthless of mankind." He walked bent forward, De Quincey said, at his worst in a state of motion, a tall gaunt man like Don Quixote, his legs not ornamental but thick and ill-shaped, his narrow shoulders drooping.

However he looked walking, Wordsworth must have made a disconcerting companion to walk with, since he composed aloud, mouthing and muttering his verse. He himself guessed that nine-tenths of his poems had been murmured out in the open air. The neighbors called it his booing about. One of them remarked, "He goes bumming and muffing, and talking to hissen, but *whiles* he's as sensible as you or me." At Racedown the country people grew suspicious of his sanity. He carried a pocket telescope that they feared he used to bewitch the cattle.

With Dorothy silent at his side (stooping and companionably bent like him as she walked), he composed the whole of "Tintern Abbey" in his head, muffing and booing along for four or five days in July, 1798. He kept at it from the time they left Tintern, crossed the river Wye, returned twice more to Tintern for another look at the scenery, and walked on—till he finally ended, on a note of benediction to his sister ("thou my dearest Friend"), one evening just as they entered Bristol.

"Not a line of it was altered and not any part of it written down till I reached Bristol," he said. The poem has 159 lines.

Yet there were other times when Wordsworth waited to recollect his turbulent emotion in tranquillity. He delayed two years in writing about the daffodils, a little overlong as it proved, for he began forgetful: "I wandered lonely as a cloud," an extraordinary thing to say when Dorothy strode right beside him on that immortal walk. He wasn't lonely, and the cloud wasn't lonely. Since it was a dark stormy day, getting ready to rain, the sky must have been full of clouds.

They weren't wandering, either. Dorothy says the date was April 15, 1802, when, returning from Eusemere after visiting the Clarksons, they came at Ullswater upon the spectacle—"Look, William, the daffodils!" She gave him eyes, she gave him ears, and he took all the credit:

> Ten thousand saw I at a glance,
> Tossing their heads in sprightly dance.

Dorothy would never in her life exaggerate like that. Ten *thousand?* She looked facts in the face, noted with accuracy, and stated in her journal:

When we were in the woods beyond Gowborrow Park we saw a few daffodils close to the water-side. . . . But as we went along there were more and yet more; and at last, under the boughs of the trees, we saw that there was a long belt of them along the shore, about the breadth of a country turnpike road. I never saw daffodils so beautiful. They grew among the mossy stones about and about them; some rested their heads upon these stones as on a pillow for weariness; and the rest tossed and reeled and danced, and seemed as if they verily laughed with the wind, that blew upon them over the lake: they looked so gay, ever glancing, ever changing.

Then, as she went on to say, the storm broke and it started to rain. "The wind was furious." Wordsworth chose to call it a breeze.

A Walk with John Chester

On a spring day in 1798, the weather was good. "We set off together on foot," wrote Hazlitt in his essay "My First Acquaintance with Poets"—"Coleridge, John Chester, and I." And who was this John Chester? "This Chester was a native of Nether Stowey, one of those who were attracted to Coleridge's discourse as flies are to honey. . . . He had on a brown cloth coat, boots, and corduroy breeches, was low in stature, bow-legged, had a drag in his walk like a drover, which he assisted by a hazel switch, and kept on a sort of trot by the side of Coleridge, like a running footman by a state coach, that he might not lose a syllable or sound, that fell from Coleridge's lips, much less offered an opinion the whole way: yet of the three, had I to chuse during that journey, I would be John Chester."

It was a long day's journey, exhausting but momentous for twenty-year-old Hazlitt, with his two bemused companions, one completely silent, one completely voluble—from the tiny village of Nether Stowey in the Quantock hills where Coleridge lived for three years, down the Bristol Channel to Lynton by the sea. They took the high road that dipped to Minehead, passing Dunster on their right, watching the lovely coast scenery (at least Hazlitt watched), for miles and miles while "our feet kept time to the echoes of Coleridge's tongue," and the sun set and darkness came. And John Chester only listened.

Not till midnight did they reach Lynton, find lodging, and eat at that hour a supper of bacon and eggs. Sitting at table with his idol, John Chester was happy. His happiness was well repaid. Though a thunderstorm competed with him, Coleridge talked serenely on and, next morning at breakfast, continued to talk. He passed judgment on Virgil's *Georgics*, compared Shakespeare and Milton, spoke tolerantly of Pope but not of his versification, expressed dislike of Dr. Johnson, contempt for Gray (and, years later, contempt for Hazlitt: "His manners are 99 in a 100 singularly repulsive"). Hazlitt found him both profound and perverse.

"He be a wunnerful man, thik Coleridge," whispered Chester, tugging at Hazlitt's sleeve.

Beyond the fact that Chester revealed the country name of a seaweed as they loitered by the shore, no further eloquence from him is reported. When Coleridge set out for Germany with the Wordsworths that fall, on September 14, 1798, who should be in their company but John Chester, still tagging doglike along. Coleridge had requested that his friend join them. Dorothy mentions his presence several times in her journal of the tour, but as usual he is unquoted, being speechless: "Hamburg, September 20, 1798. Chester and I went to the promenade . . . after spending two hours very pleasantly we returned home."

Ten days later, Coleridge and his dumb friend left the Wordsworths and traveled on alone in Germany where, Hazlitt guessed, "the Kantean philosophers were puzzled how to bring him under any of their categories." John Chester was supposed to be there to study German agriculture, but he may have omitted to say so.

They stayed for a while in Ratzeburg, where Coleridge was bitterly unhappy and homesick, though the record shows that Chester spoke aloud twice. Once he greeted Coleridge with the words, "No letters from England." A second time, when a letter came at last from Sara left behind in Nether Stowey, Chester said, "Why don't you read the letter?" And Coleridge read it.

In February they went on to Göttingen. From time to time Coleridge wrote in tears to his two dearest companions, Dorothy and William, crying out his loss and his utter loneliness: "You have all in each other, but I am lonely, and want you!"

Yet always trotting at his side was the figure of John Chester from Somerset, bowlegged, inarticulate, and worshipful, to whom Coleridge owed by now five pounds and twelve shillings.

I Would Be John Chester

"I would be John Chester,"
Says Hazlitt. Of the three
Who walked from Nether Stowey
Past Dunster by the sea—
Two and the mighty Coleridge,
His towering words set free—
Silent was John Chester,
Listening manfully.

From that torrential fancy
No sheltering had they
Through Minehead on to Lynton.
Soliloquy by day,
By darkness overtaken,
Digressed their life away.
And silent walked John Chester
Without a word to say.

Yet naturally I wonder
What more he might have done,
Watching the seagulls wheeling,
Marking the vanished sun.
John Chester only listened
Once Coleridge had begun.
And I would be John Chester,
And so would anyone.

Ben Jonson, Walker

In the summer of 1618 Ben Jonson, forty-six, weighing nearly twenty stone (280 pounds), walked the four hundred miles from London to Edinburgh. Francis Bacon had told him he should go on poetic feet, dactyls and spondees, but Jonson chose to lumber off on two feet of his own. It took him a month, traveling the North Road through Yorkshire and Northumberland, and at Durham he stopped to buy a new pair of shoes.

One day his huge bulky figure, "my mountain belly and my rocky face," turned up at Hawthornden, an estate seven miles from Edinburgh. (John Aubrey said he had one eye lower and bigger than the other. Thomas Dekker said his face looked like a rotten russet apple when it was bruised. A most ungodly face, Dekker said.) There he stayed two or three weeks, talking his head off and drinking Drummond's excellent wine. "Swell me a bowl with lusty wine," Jonson probably recited,

> I drink as I would write
> In flowing measure, filled with flame and sprite

and drank the cellar dry. Drink was an element in which he lived, observed his host afterward.

William Drummond waited under a sycamore tree when Jonson arrived. According to legend, Drummond cried, "Welcome, welcome, royal Ben!" to which Jonson promptly replied, "Thank ye, thank ye, Hawthornden." From that moment, Drummond, a polite, gentle, earnest, sober bachelor in his thirties, had but to listen—what else could he do? He was no match for Ben. In tireless monologue the great London poet (pensioned by King James and in effect the first poet laureate) aired his views, gossiped about everyone of importance, told bawdy tales, roared, reminisced about his love affairs ("O, if a man could restrain the fury of his gullet and groin"), called his wife a shrew but honest whom he had not "bedded with" for five years, and launched at length upon the story of his life.

"A bragger," said Drummond to himself and wrote it into his notebook.

Jonson in his cups spoke ill of everybody. He declared that Spenser's stanzas pleased him not ("Spenser writ no language"), Shakespeare wanted art, Donne deserved hanging for not keeping of accent and would perish. He cursed Petrarch. He advised Drummond to abandon poetry, being too simple a man to practice it.

"In his merry humour," noted Drummond, "he was wont to name himself 'The Poet.' "

Jonson hated bricklaying, he announced, and music with his meals. He liked couplets. When Drummond showed him his large scholar's library, "Read Quintilian!" thundered Ben. He gossiped about the late Queen, who never saw herself after she became old in a true looking glass. "They painted her and sometimes would vermilion her nose."

Shaking with laughter, his belly bouncing at his own wit ("Room! room! make room for the bouncing Belly! Hail, hail, plump paunch!"), he told about a man who lit his pipe with a ballad and next day had a singing in his head. About a man who let his hair grow long to see if it would go to seed. About a lady who so admired a Mr. Dod, a Puritan preacher, that she asked her husband if she might lie with Mr. Dod and so conceive by him a heavenly angel or a saint. Permission was granted. When the infant of this union was born, it came into the world just an ordinary child.

As hospitality required, the weary Drummond held his tongue and passed the canary. After his guest weaved off to bed having ranted the night away (unaware all this loose talk was being carefully recorded), Drummond stayed up to write the lot into his journal—the gossip, the scandal, the nonsense—which ironically was published after his death as *Conversations*. At times he sounds jarred and offended, like a man who has lost sleep, endured and heard too much. When the visit was at last over and Jonson on his merry way, he turned again to his notes.

"He is a great lover and praiser of himself," wrote Drummond, calling him a few more names: a disparager, a dissembler, a blasphemer, one who would rather lose a friend than a jest, "a contemner and scorner of others."

"By God, 'tis good," was Ben Jonson's own view of his poetry (and of himself), "and if you like't, you may." How did he get his 280 pounds the four hundred miles back to London? He walked.

Herrick's Julia

I worry about Julia. She was the lady of his heart, to whom Herrick addressed some seventy love poems, calling her "prime of all." Whatever others say, I believe she was a real live girl. But then, weren't the rest real too, "My many fresh and fragrant mistresses"? It hardly sounds as if Herrick meant only the imaginary women of his dreams.

The list is long, a staggering number for an English cleric to woo and adore. They were, by my count,

> Irene, Oenone, Anthea, Corinna,
> Dianeme, Perilla, and Perenna,
> Electra, Julia, Lucia, Amarillis,
> Biancha, Myrrha, Silvia, Sapho, Phillis,

which adds up to sixteen names, all classical, besides several more with last names and identities, like Thomasin and Dorothy Parsons, daughters of the organist of Westminster Abbey; Amy Potter, daughter of his predecessor at Dean Prior; Mistress Dorothy Kennedy, from whom he parted as a lover sadly noting his tears.

One critic explains these ladies as "Either a score of pretty girls (or one girl under a score of names)." Edmund Gosse believed in the reality of Julia but not of Perilla, Silvia, Anthea, and the rest. However it was, Herrick remains a bewildering love poet, about whom Julia had reasonable cause for alarm. For one thing, since there is no order in the arrangement of his poems and no chronology, he appears to leap faithless and forgetful from one love affair to the next, from passionate youth to tired old age, from London to Dean Prior, from lust to chastity, from desire to rejection of desire. These are not mere shifts of mood: they are contradictions of fact. He is unfaithful and he is true. He loves and he loves not.

In "No Spouse but a Sister," he swears he will remain forever chaste, he will stay a bachelor

> And never take a wife
> To crucify my life.

In "Single Life Most Secure," he will avoid for his part the discontent and strife of marriage. In "Upon Himself," he says, "I could never love indeed,"

> I could never seek to please
> One, or many mistresses.

In "To his Tomb-maker," he orders these celibate words carved on the stone:

> Chaste I liv'd, without a wife,
> That's the story of my life.
> Strewings need none, every flower
> Is in this word, Bachelor.

But did Herrick really live chaste, "my neck from love's yoke free"? Or did he live, again in his own words, "wisely wanton," in "cleanly wantonness"? He was an attractive man from his picture, with a mop of curly black hair, a mustache, a fleshly face that could be lustful enough. Or, I suppose, pious.

When a man writes as many as 1,400 verses, he is likely to say a number of contradictory things, as Herrick did even in a single poem, "The Poet Loves a Mistress, but Not to Marry,"

> I do not love to wed
> Though I do like to woo.
> And for a maidenhead
> I'll beg, and buy it too.

During his twenty years as a country parson in the tiny hamlet of Dean Prior (in dull Devonshire he "loathed so much"), Herrick called it a place of banishment and exile where "More discontents I never had / Since I was born than here." Its people were churls, rude as rudest savages, and once he threw his sermon at the congregation, cursing them for sleeping. Yet Herrick often wrote with rapture of "His Content in the Country," blessing his good fortune and good life. He sang, a happy country man, "of brooks, of blossoms, birds and bowers," and made in Devon his lovely meadow verse, "Here in green meadows sits eternal May."

Here he lived genial and domesticated, a man of simple tastes, in the company of a lamb, a cat, a teeming hen, a goose, a cow, a spaniel named Tracy, a sparrow named Phil, a pet pig who drank ale from his tankard, a bed of tulips, and a faithful housekeeper to tend him, Prudence Baldwin, "my Prue." He thanked God for his little house, his little buttery, his little loaf of bread (a little watercress and beets besides): "They well content my Prue and me."

Where, oh where, in that snug rectory, full of sermons, pets, and books, did Herrick find room for all those mistresses?

Yet there is Julia.

Also, there is Phillis, whom he invites to share the country with him: "Live, live with me, and thou shalt see / The pleasures I'll prepare for thee."

And Perilla, whom he gives his "supremest kiss." When he is dead, she is to be at his side to wind him

in that very sheet
Which wrapt thy smooth limbs (when thou didst implore
The Gods' protection, but the night before).

And Perenna: "when I thy parts run o'er,"

> the more I look, the more I prove,
> There's still more cause why I the more should love.

And Lucia, of whom he asks a kiss and wonders what would have happened had he then asked for her maidenhead. Once he dreamed he was a grape vine creeping over her, till he woke

> And found (ah me!) this flesh of mine
> More like a stock than like a vine.

And Dianeme, whose finger he sucks when a bee stings her, though she lets him bleed for love. Dianeme, he cries,

> Show me thy feet; show me thy legs, thy thighs;
> Show me those *Fleshly Principalities;*
> Show me that hill (where smiling Love doth sit)
> Having a living fountain under it.
> Show me thy waist; then let me there withall
> By the *assention* of thy lawn, see all.

And Biancha, whose heady perfume leads where he must follow.

And Oenone: "For shame or pity now incline / To play the loving part."

And Sapho, a "principal" mistress: "Let us now take time and play / Love, and live here while we may."

And Silvia: "I confess, / My kiss out-went the bounds of shamefastness." So,

> Let us (though late) at last (my Silvia) wed,
> And loving, lie in one devoted bed.

And Anthea: "When in bed she lies" and when he kisses Anthea's breasts, lips, hands, legs, thighs, she is the one "who may command him anything,"

> Thou art my life, my love, my heart,
> The very eyes of me:
> And hath command of every part,
> To live and die for thee.

And Corinna, whom he loves for her wit; and Myrrha, for her singing voice. At the thought of Irene, he freezes and fries. And so on.

In fact, he loves them all. In "Love Dislikes Nothing," Herrick protests his encompassing general love:

> Whatsoever thing I see
> Rich or poor although it be;
> 'Tis a Mistress unto me.

His invitations to bed sound not only urgent but honest: "Lovesick I am," a man for every scene of love, no trifler but sensual and naked in desire. Let them be Lucrece by day, Thais by night, he would renew his strength only to pleasure them. And, in return, let them neither "Famish me, nor over-fill."

In "To His Mistresses," Herrick laments his advancing years, "Old I am, and cannot do / That, I was accustom'd to." He asks his girls to work their magic spells and bring to his thighs, arms, and legs "their former heat." He invites his dearest beauties to gather at his tomb, where he will cast on them a loving eye, sighing because he has lost the world too soon, "and in it, you the most."

Yet there is Julia, most of all Julia.

Herrick knows her so very intimately and well. He knows her breasts where his lips may lie:

> Display thy breasts, my Julia, there let me
> Behold that circummortal purity,

and the nipples of her breasts, like a strawberry half drowned in cream. He knows her mouth, her lips, her breath where all the spices of the East are circumfused, her teeth white as Zenobia's, her skin like lawn, her black eyes, her high forehead, her nose, her double chin (would Herrick invent that?), her hair, her sweat, her waist, her dainty leg "white and hairless as an egg," her tempestuous petticoat, her silvery voice, her blushes, her tears.

He knows her everywhere, "in each thy dainty and peculiar part." He knows Julia unlacing herself, knows her bed "plump, soft, and swelling," and he touches her body with love—"My soul I'll pour into thee."

I worry about Julia. I assume she *was* real, not fancied or yearned for but real. And when she read the endless impassioned love verses he addressed to other mistresses, I hope she laughed heartily. "Dear Herrick," I hope she said, "what a lover! always forgetting what pretty name he called me yesterday." Like Electra.

To Electra

I'll come to thee in all those shapes
As Jove did, when he made his rapes:
Only, I'll not appear to thee
As he did once to Semele.
Thunder and lightning I'll lay by,
To talk with thee familiarly.
Which done, then quickly we'll undress
To one and th'others nakedness.
And ravished, plunge into the bed,
(Bodies and souls commingled)
And kissing, so as none may hear,
We'll weary all the Fables there.

Herrick published his poems when he was fifty-seven, and perhaps until his death in Devon he wrote no more verse thereafter. His last request to Julia was in the nature of a confession, "I have been wanton, and too bold I fear,"

> Beg for my pardon, Julia; he doth win
> Grace with the Gods, who's sorry for his sin.

But then, for whatever reason, he closed the *Hesperides* with this amazing couplet:

> To his Book's end this last line he'd have placed,
> *Jocund his Muse was; but his life was chaste.*

FINIS

The Suitor of Christina Rossetti

He looked a pedantic little man, shrinking of manner, with large blue nearsighted eyes that blinked—a frail little man with a high forehead and shuffling gait. He first came to the Rossetti house in London to take Italian lessons from Christina's father, though Mr. Charles Bagot Cayley already knew Arabic and Urdu and was proficient in Iroquois.

Soon he was paying morning calls on Christina, wooing her in an absent, wistful fashion that touched her heart. A woolgathering lover, given to making learned puns, even these he offered with a self-effacing, mid-Victorian air that she found endearing.

The courtship had a singular charm. Christina always dressed in black. Mr. Cayley wore a rumpled shirt without collar and an old tailcoat. Once he brought her a sea mouse swimming in spirits, accompanied by a few scholarly notes on sea mice. (She kept the mouse all her life, and wrote a poem about it, "A Venus seems my mouse.") Once he cut out a paragraph from the London *Times* on wombats and presented it to her. She called him "My blindest buzzard. My special mole."

After five years of yearning, he proposed and she rejected him. His was a hopeless passion to which by now he was probably resigned. Christina had reached a devout thirty-six, "Too late for love, too late for joy," and Mr. Cayley as a freethinker would never do. Her Christian duty was to give him up, which she did, trusting to meet him in a reformed state in a better world.

Painful as the renunciation was for them both, he con-

tinued to make frequent visits and often came to dinner or
to play whist, while she went to find him immersed in books
in the British Museum. In his letters he addressed her with
decorum as "Dear Miss Christina Rossetti," and would
sometimes discuss correct English usage. After more than
twenty years of constant devotion with never a word of re-
proach, he paid her the courtesy of dying on her birthday,
December 5, 1883.

Gentle Christina, gentle Mr. Cayley—they would have
made a charming pair, she the shyest of women as he was
of men. Edmund Gosse said of her, "Her character was so
retiring as to be almost invisible." She lacked gaiety, just
as she lacked a good ear when she wrote "O love songs
gurgling from a hundred throats." Grief was her element,
more congenial, deeper than delight. Though it seems need-
lessly grim of her, she did insist on martyrdom.

F. L. Lucas said that Christina knew few things but knew
them well; one thing she knew was her own mind. If this
is true, it brought her anguish, the rejection of love, the
horror of the grave. What she didn't know perhaps was her
own heart. Whichever it was prompted her to elect celibacy
for them both, loneliness and no marriage bed, she loved
this unworldly shabby scholar so much in need of her love:

> I love you and you know it—this at least,
> This comfort is mine own in all my pain;
> You know it, and can never doubt again.

She loved Mr. Cayley and, woman and poet, she told
him so. Only she loved God more. "I love Him more," she
said, "so let me love you too."

Mr. Cayley

I hear that he was shy, a timorous suitor,
Affectionate by nature, man and boy,
But deep-abstracted, given to grave employments
Like turning the Gospels into Iroquois.

A little odd and philological
For love was Mr. Cayley, even prim
To fill the role of mid-Victorian lover,
Though as such did Miss Rossetti fancy him.

At wooing he was mild, I think—his features
Look rather pinched for passion, forehead bare,
Too cerebral for world or flesh or devil
To have left a flickering impression there.

Yet it may be that love turned Cayley giddy,
Brazen at times and bolstered by delight.
The evidence is small. His way with women
One dare not place in too intense a light.

Still, there it was, a gay pre-Raphaelite party
Where, taken by Christina, ill at ease,
The poor man hid for hours behind the greenery,
Composing a few passing pleasantries.

At last he hurried forth in buckled armor
And stayed two ladies, flowingly attired.
To each he bowed, a trifle wan but valiant.
"Are you interested in the Gulf Stream?" he inquired.

In the end, of course, Christina wed nobody
But clung unwavering to her spinsterhood.
It saddens me to own that his fine bravura
Never did Mr. Cayley any good.

Rabelais on Marriage

The monk Rabelais who loved wine and laughter never married, though he had a natural son Théodule and possibly two more children. Out of his wisdom, out of *le rire immense* (what is larger than that laughter?), he inspired Pantagruel to give his friend Panurge sound guidance on the subject "Is marriage advisable?" He was the perfect marriage counselor.

Panurge began in this fashion: Maybe one ought to stay a bachelor rather than rush headlong into a hairbrained undertaking like marriage.

Quoth Pantagruel, "Then do not marry."

But, argued Panurge, I would be solitary without a wife. I would have only myself, not the joy and solace of wedlock.

"Then marry, in the name of God," quoth Pantagruel.

Suppose my wife proved unfaithful. Fond as I am of cuckolds, I don't want to be numbered among them.

"Then do not marry," quoth Pantagruel. "What thou to others shalt have done, others will do the like to thee."

But since I can't live without a wife, shouldn't I find a virtuous woman to be true to me? Changing females every day, I've never yet enjoyed an honest woman who was another man's wife.

"Marry then, in God's name," quoth Pantagruel.

On the other hand, an honest woman might be ill-tempered and beat me, in which case I would have to hit her back.

"Do not marry then," quoth Pantagruel.

That way I'll have no one to love me. Suppose I fall sick? Who will look after me?

"Marry then, in the name of God," quoth Pantagruel.

Yet if I fall sick and haven't the strength to make love to my wife, she may turn to the embraces of another man.

"Do not marry then," quoth Pantagruel.

If I don't I'll have no lawful sons and daughters to perpetuate my name and leave my fortune to (when I acquire one). What consolations have the unmarried? Only scoffs and mockery.

"Marry then, in the name of God," quoth Pantagruel.

Pantagruel was only following the motto of the Abbey of Thélème, *Fais ce que voudrais.* Truly the rascal Panurge never got better advice, though heaven knows he tried. Still wobbling in doubt, he consulted his dreams, then the dice, both of which could be interpreted to mean he would be made a cuckold if he married, or else he would not. He visited the Sibyl of Panzoust who, stirring a pot of cabbage soup, made a prophecy that so terrified him he cried out, "I will not marry; no, believe me, I will not." He asked for a sign from Goatsnose, a deaf-mute, who signaled Panurge he would be married, cuckolded, beaten, and robbed. He consulted a poet, Raminagrobis, a jolly old man who happened to be dying but produced a poem anyway: "Take, or not take her / Off, or on." A magician, Herr Trippa, affirmed Panurge's fate to be cuckoldry, which is unavoidable. "The devil take him!" said Panurge, turning to Friar John, who advised, "Marry in the devil's name. Why not?"

For his next source of wisdom, Panurge went to a theologian, Hippothadeus, who assured him he would not be cuckolded if it pleased God, or if it pleased God he would. A doctor, Rondibilis, whom he asked "Shall I marry or not?", discussed learnedly the fervency of lust and offered Panurge five ways of curbing it. Copulation was one way. But cuckoldry, he said, is a natural appendage of marriage. Nature lost her senses when she made women. The philosopher Trouillogan replied with shifts and evasions to his questions: "Shall I marry?" "I have no hand in it." "Then shall I not marry?" "I cannot help it." He seemed to say that Panurge ought to do neither one. Or both.

His friend Pantagruel finally persuaded Panurge the wisest thing to do was to take counsel of a fool. On the way they stopped at a court of justice to hear Judge Bridlegoose, whose answers were as simpleminded and inscrutable as the law. The fool Triboullet said Panurge was a fool to marry. Both of them therefore were fools, sots, noodles, and loons. "The whole world is foolish," observed Panurge.

So he resolved to complete his quest and visit the Oracle of the Holy Bottle, where the solution must lie. After going to sea and wandering in unknown lands of fantasy, he reached the Temple of the Holy Bottle, where the high priestess BacBuc brought Panurge before the Bottle itself. There he drank the divine liquor and it went down like mother's milk. (Rabelais was a lover of wine: "I drink no more than a sponge.") Truth is in wine, said BacBuc; the answer lies within: "Form your own judgment, reach your own conclusions. Be yourself the expounder of your understanding."

She's right, said Pantagruel. This, you remember, was the sane advice he gave Panurge in the first place.

And, lecher that he was, no doubt Panurge did go ahead and marry. Like everyone else.

Miss Cassandra Austen

Cassandra had a fine aristocratic nose, like her mother for whom she was named. She had black eyes and a sweet temper, and she was three years older than Jane (whose eyes were hazel, whose temper was spirited).

How little one knows of her, yet how much because of Jane. The sisters were called equally sensible. They slept together, walked together, spent their lives together at Steventon Rectory or at Chawton Cottage sixteen miles away, till Jane died at forty-two in Cassandra's arms. Jane would read aloud to her sister what she had written, and Cassandra would burst into fits of laughter.

Jane's letters to Cassandra (over a period of twenty-one years during their brief separations, say, when Cassandra went to visit brother Edward at Godmersham Park) begin in 1796. Jane was twenty years old, Cassandra twenty-three. In the next year, 1797, Thomas Fowle to whom Cassandra was engaged died of yellow fever in the West Indies.

Nothing of this tragedy appears in Jane's letters. None of Cassandra's answers to her sister survive. After Jane's death, Cassandra burned all of the intimate ones she had received from Jane, and with a pair of scissors snipped out whole passages, or sometimes a single word, from others. She deleted and pruned. It was exasperating of her. In the midst of Jane's description of a pretty colored muslin with small red dots, of which she had bought ten yards at 3/6, a line will have been cut away.

Such a correspondence naturally contained many revelations and some griefs. "I tell you everything," Jane wrote. If she made outcry, as she must have done, if she was ever in love as she probably was, Cassandra suppressed it. She wanted no word left that would warrant their publication. Nothing intimate or private or even interesting was to remain.

She did infinite harm, of course, however good her intentions. Though Jane herself well knew how tremendously valuable is the data of life, Cassandra did not. Blindly, wilfully, she destroyed the data. As a result, the critics, in particular male critics (like E. M. Forster disdainful and Sir Harold Nicolson bored—he thought Cassandra "as a woman, immeasurably dull"), have been quick to find the letters silly and empty twaddle, without event or fact. But what of the missing ones? Cassandra got rid of a great many, the best of them, because they sounded too personal, too real; because they were confidences and told too much.

One knows her now by what Jane is not allowed to say. Prudent Cassandra, the silent one, the censor: the wonder is she didn't burn every line. The wonder is what she left should be so entertaining. In spite of her damage, the letters are full of marvelous nonsense and teasing, light gossip, laughter, and love. Jane called Cassandra "the finest comic writer of the present age," though how true the claim is we can never know.

In a reflected light she lives and breathes, in tantalizing glimpses. Cassandra painted watercolor portraits, Jane wrote. They read novels. They always wore a cap, two neat sisters who disliked tousle and untidiness. They were good at needlework, especially overcast and satin stitch. Both were pretty, above middle height, blushed easily, loved clothes, loved to dance. Both were poor spellers, but with a difference: Jane laughingly accused Cassandra of adding a vowel wherever she could, whereas Jane reversed her vowels (adeiu, beleive, peice, neice, veiw, cheif, releif, greif). She was quite consistent about it, beginning with her first book, *Love and Freindship*.

Of the two, Cassandra's face was said to be more regularly handsome, and Jane thought her a better person, wiser than herself. She was more reserved, conservative, cautious, more discreet than Jane, who alludes to her sister's starched notions.

But they were equally good-tempered, amiable, loving. They seemed not to scold or disagree, only to confide, to amuse each other. Each knew the other's mind. Jane's playful wit was answered by wit. As she thanks Cassandra for being so amusing and one reads the lost letter with her, Cassandra almost emerges from the shadows, face alight, a smile in her dark eyes.

From Jane to Cassandra, September 1, 1796: "The letter which I have this moment received from you has diverted me beyond moderation. I could die of laughter at it."

November 25, 1798: "I am sure nobody can desire your letters as much as I do, and I don't think anybody deserves them so well."

December 18, 1798: "I have changed my mind, and changed the trimmings of my cap this morning; they are now such as you suggested; I felt as if I should not prosper if I strayed from your directions."

January 21, 1799: "Your letter has pleased and amused me very much. . . . You quite abash me by your progress in notting, for I am still without silk."

November 1, 1800: "Your abuse of our gowns amuses, but does not discourage me. I wore at the ball your favourite gown, a bit of muslin of the same round my head, bordered with Mrs. Cooper's band and one little comb."

January 14, 1801: "It gives us great pleasure to know

that the Chilham Ball was so agreeable and that you danced four dances with Mr. Kemble. . . . Why did you dance four dances with so stupid a man?"

October 13, 1813: "Your self-reproach on the subject of Mrs. Stockwell made me laugh heartily. . . . I had not heard before of her having the measles."

October 26, 1813: "I long to know whether you are buying stockings or what you are doing."

My dearest Cassandra, she wrote, with "infinities of love." Almost the last letter Jane sent to anyone before the illness from which she died was to thank her sister for being all that she was. "Yours was a treasure, so full of everything."

Only two brief heartbroken letters remain of those Cassandra wrote—both of them to her niece Fanny Knight after Jane's death to speak of the loss of her other self: "She was the sun of my life. . . . I had not a thought concealed from her. . . . I loved her only too well."

Cassandra and Jane

The prettier Miss Austen of the two
Cassandra was, the older girl. A few,
Like Jane herself, believed her the more wise
And talented sister. But it's hard to tell
About someone who stays invisible.
"I always loved Cassandra for her dark eyes,"

Jane said, and with a word or two of Jane's
She haunts the mind: a pretty girl with brains,
The quiet one—and now forever quiet—
The one who never trifled with her pen
Or spoke her heart and scribbled it again,
Having no wish perhaps to clarify it.

Yet how alike they were. They seemed to share
A life almost, inseparable as a pair,
Who laughed and talked and dearly loved a ball
(Lord Portsmouth gave a ball), or paid the three
Miss Biggs of Manydown Park and formally
Were paid (Jane wrote down afterward) a call:

"They came & they sat & they went." Like this the days
Passed in routine, with household tasks, with ways
To boil a chicken tender, endless talk
Of velvet bonnets or a muslin gown,
Poor Mrs. Lance, the gossip of the town,
The pleasures of a book, a country walk—

Cassandra, Jane. Except, once in a while,
Jane sewing by the fire would pause and smile,

Jump up and run across the room to write
Words at her desk. Then silent as before,
She would return to her embroidery or
Glance at Cassandra, sewing by lamplight.

It was the only difference—a small
Habit of Jane's, not troublesome at all,
Of scribbling things she met with, noted, heard.
And the real way of telling them apart
Was only this: Jane spoke and revealed her heart.
Cassandra listened, saying not a word.

The Way to Little Gidding

It was still winterspring in England, a cold rainy day in early April, and the bus I took, No. 151 to Peterborough, was a big red double-decker like the London buses. Nobody in it looked as if he were making a pilgrimage.

T. S. Eliot says in the *Four Quartets* that you go to Little Gidding from wherever you are. And it is here, in England and nowhere. "If you came this way, / Taking the route you would be likely to take / From the place you would be likely to come from"—you would find it. The place I was likely to come from was Cambridge, since that's where I was, only a few miles from Huntingdonshire where Little Gidding was supposed to be. Yet nobody I asked (at the hotel desk, the bus terminal, the railroad station) had ever heard of it. There was no train connection. I decided to take the Peterborough bus and see how close I could come.

The conductor, puzzled by my destination, offered to consult the bus driver. He returned to say he would try putting me off this side of Peterborough at a crossroads near Alconbury. Scratching his head, he went to have another talk with the driver. A minute later he came back to say they had decided on a different crossroads farther on. I asked him point-blank:

"Do you know where Little Gidding is?"

"Not actually, no. Can't say I do," he replied.

"If you came this way, taking the route you would be likely to take, is this the route you would take, do you think?"

"Well now, that I can't rightly say. It could be."

"What about the driver? Does he know where Little Gidding is?"

"He says it might be somewhat near to Great Gidding."

I didn't ask him if he had ever heard of T. S. Eliot.

Lambing was over in Cambridgeshire, and the fields we passed were full of baby lambs frisking beside their mothers. The conductor stopped at my seat a third time to assure me he and the driver had the problem licked. He would put me off just beyond Alconbury Hill.

"That should be about six miles from there over to the Giddings," he said kindly, "however you went about it."

We rode on in the rain into Huntingdonshire, passing again through the little village of Godmanchester I had visited on this same bus only last week. I didn't yet know how to pronounce Godmanchester, whether the accent was on man or God. But I reflected I had now traveled in England to Chester, to Manchester, and to Godmanchester, which should bring me to the end of the prefixes unless there was a Goodgodmanchester somewhere as well. Beyond the town of Huntingdon, the county seat, we joined the Great North Road from London. This side of Alconbury Hill, twenty-three miles from Cambridge, the conductor came to lean over my shoulder, scanning the road ahead.

"Can't be far off now, can we?" he said, breathing hard on my neck. "I mean, it has to be hereabouts, hasn't it?" He rang the bell and cordially helped me off at Conington crossroads.

A small wooden sign pointed cross-country to the left:

Great Gidding—4 miles
Little Gidding—5¼ miles

My appetite for this journey had by now considerably waned. To walk some eleven miles back and forth across a flat, forsaken English countryside in the pouring rain appealed not at all, not even for Mr. Eliot's sake. I looked around for help and spotted a pub across the double highway, the Crown and Woolpack, where over half a bitter I might consider a way to make this literary pilgrimage in reasonable comfort.

My instinct was right—the innkeeper had a solution. He had never visited Little Gidding himself ("I haven't lived in these parts but ten years," he said) and showed no curiosity as to why one would elect to seek it out. But he listened thoughtfully. "That'll do it," he said, "the man from Sawtry," and went to the telephone.

Within ten minutes, the man from Sawtry arrived in his ancient Ford car. A Deliverer, you might say, in the Eliot tradition. Though he had a terrible stutter (Eliot missed a trick here), he conveyed the idea as I climbed gratefully in that there were not two but *three* Giddings over yonder, and which one did I want?

"Little Gidding," I said. "Have you been to Little Gidding?"

"I s-s-h-h-h-houldn't think so, ma'am."

"Is there a church there, do you think?"

"One's at S-s-s-s-steeple Gidding."

The country road lay quiet in the rain, with lots of graceful winding turns. Four miles distant, we reached Great Gidding, a sleepy hamlet of yellow stone houses and, the man from Sawtry guessed, about three hundred inhabitants. At noon not a soul stirred.

More than a mile beyond, we came to a small sign beside the road: "Little Gidding Only." No houses were in sight within the thick grove of beeches, but the sign clearly pointed to the right to a narrow muddy lane, lined with potato bags hanging on the fences. This we followed in low gear for a half-mile to where the lane came to an abrupt end in a farmer's barnyard. Beyond we could see a pond and a green countryside, nothing more. Two large barns,

one on either side of the road, effectually hid the farmhouse.

The man from Sawtry turned in his seat to know if I
was well pleased with the trip.

"Where are we?" I asked.

He looked about him in surprise and shook his head. He
didn't know.

"This barnyard doesn't look like Little Gidding to me,"
I said. "Maybe we aren't there yet, would you say?"

Agreeing we couldn't be, he backed the car out of the
barnyard, maneuvered a turnaround, and drove down the
potholed lane the way we had come. We went whizzing
up the country road a mile farther, till we reached another
road sign: "Steeple Gidding Only." Here again we turned
as directed and followed a muddy lane to its end. Behind
a picket fence stood a little gray stone church, surrounded
by old elms and fallen gravestones in the small churchyard.

I got out and went inside the cold bleak church with
its dozen pews and altar, but there was no sign of what I
sought, nothing but a dim memorial to Sir John Cotton,
1752. In perplexity I returned to the guide and shrugged.

"No?" he said.

"No, this isn't Little Gidding. I think it must be Steeple
Gidding, don't you?"

The man from Sawtry looked crestfallen, and for a
while we stood uncertainly in the rain wondering what to
do. An idea came to him. "I'll ask!" he cried and ran off
through the field to a farmhouse hidden by trees, hurrying
back almost at once with a broad smile. "Get in," he said.
He was a man of few words.

We drove hellbent back to the sign "Little Gidding
Only," turned in at the now familiar lane, and splashed

our way to the farmer's barnyard. This time on reaching
the dead end we kept on a few feet farther, past the barns
into the farmer's grassy field. From there we could gaze
into his chicken yard. Beyond it, on the other side of the
chicken coop, stood Little Gidding.

> If you came by day not knowing what you came for,
> It would be the same, when you leave the rough road
> And turn behind the pig-sty to the dull façade
> And the tombstone.

The incredibly tiny church was gray stone, its façade
weathered and dull. A bell hung in the small steeple; great
elms and a beech wood spread behind. Halfway down the
flagstone path stood the tombstone, the simple gray tomb of
Nicholas Ferrar. Over the door of Ferrar's church shone
the words, "This is none other but the House of God and
the Gate of Heaven."

Inside, it gleamed like a bright jewel, with shining brass
font (out of which cattle used to drink) and eagle lectern
(hurled into the pond by the Puritans), an altar of cedar-
wood, a stained-glass window of the Crucifixion, and twelve
highly polished oak choir stalls along each side of the
chancel. It could be lighted only by candles.

> You are not here to verify,
> Instruct yourself, or inform curiosity
> Or carry report. You are here to kneel
> Where prayer has been valid.

Mr. Eliot traveled here from London during World War
II, on a journey to the world's end, seeking peace. Nicholas
Ferrar had gone three hundred years before him for the
same reason, the cure of his soul. In 1625, Ferrar pur-
chased the dilapidated manor house of Little Gidding,

where the farmhouse now stands. The little church was being used to store hay, its floors filthy; the sacristy was a pigsty.

He brought his mother with him, his brother John, his sister Susanna, together with their families (Susanna, married to John Collett, had sixteen children)—about thirty in all who left their homes at his summons to follow him. Aged thirty-four, Nicholas was ordained deacon by Bishop Laud and entered with passion upon the religious life, seeking refuge and finding peace. Three times a day the whole family walked in procession from the house to pray in the church, which they adorned lovingly with silver-fringed tapestry cushions, rich altar hangings, a silk carpet, their own gold embroideries and exquisite bound books of Scripture. The church was made fragrant by flowers and herbs. The Book of the Psalms was repeated every twenty-four hours, with watches through the night. On Sunday the vicar of Great Gidding came over to perform the morning service. On Sunday afternoon the family walked across the fields to evensong at the church of Steeple Gidding.

And since Nicholas Ferrar, the friend of George Herbert and Richard Crashaw, had like them attended the University of Cambridge, the University students came faithfully of a Sunday for prayer and meditation. I believe they no longer do.

The fame of the holy life spread over England. King Charles I visited Little Gidding three separate times, once before the death of Ferrar, the last time as a fugitive in the dark of night, March 2, 1646. By then slander and hatred hung over the community like a cloud. It was denounced by the Puritans as monastic, a nest of Popery and secret vice. In 1641 an attack in the form of a scurrilous pamphlet, *The Arminian Nunnery*, had been circulated by the thousands and a copy presented to Parliament. In it Nicholas Ferrar was described as a superstitious priest, his nieces as nuns and virgins.

Three months after the King's last visit, the Puritan soldiers in revenge utterly destroyed the manor house and despoiled the church, ending their day's work with a huge bonfire, on which they roasted sheep killed in the grounds. Ferrar's community had lasted for twenty-two years. Then it was gone. The church was rebuilt in 1714.

The man from Sawtry, relieved as I was to find the place and complete the quest, stepped inside and couldn't believe his eyes. Dumbfounded, he swore he would bring the wife next time to have a look. I returned to Cambridge that afternoon by Bus No. 151, after being picked up on the highway and warmly welcomed by both driver and conductor as a lost-and-found American.

"Enjoyed yourself then, did you?" they asked. "Right you are."

Next day in the Cambridge library I learned from *The Survey Gazetteer of the British Isles* that the village of Little Gidding consists of a total of 42 souls. I wondered where all 42 were keeping themselves yesterday.

At Little Gidding I was reminded of J. H. Shorthouse's gentle novel *John Inglesant*, which appeared in 1880 and pleased Gladstone by its moral earnestness. The fictitious hero visited the real community of Little Gidding in the time of Charles I, discussed the "mortified life" with Nicholas Ferrar (who spent his life in mortifications and devotions), and fell hopelessly in love with Mary Collett, Ferrar's favorite niece.

The seven nieces, known (derisively in London by the wits) as the "Nuns of Gidding," were called the Patient, the Cheerful, the Affectionate, the Submiss, the Obedient, the Moderate, and the Charitable. All wore black garb and veils except John Inglesant's Mary, who as the Chief wore a friar's gray gown. Pledged to virginity, she never married him or anyone else.

A hundred little children came for instruction from the country round and were known as the "Psalm children," because at Little Gidding they were taught to love God and repeat the Psalms.

Soon after this essay, "The Way to Little Gidding," was printed in the New York *Times Book Review,* I heard from a direct descendant of the Ferrars. Her mother's name was Mary Ferrar, descended not from bachelor Nicholas but from his brother John.

She was eighty-two years old, deeply religious, unmarried, and the grandmother of seven children, having adopted two little girls long ago. Besides them, her dearest possession was a painting of the church at Little Gidding. She came from England in 1900 to live in the village of Alfred, New York, eight miles from my home town of Hornell. Had I known her when I was a little girl, she might have adopted me too. I would have cherished her company and, perhaps, there is no telling, become one of her Psalm children.

The Portrait of Oliver Cromwell

I was skeptical at first of Oliver Cromwell, believing him flawed with pride. Then about ten years ago I saw his portrait in Sidney Sussex College, Cambridge. Cromwell came there as a student in 1616, though the picture, painted when he was famous, reveals him with the warty face. "Remark all these roughnesses, pimples, warts, and everything as you see me," he told Lely, the portrait painter; "otherwise I will never pay a farthing for it." Or, in another version, "Paint me as I am, warts and all." Cromwell never in his life said anything more quotable.

Montaigne once wrote that he loved the face of Paris even to her warts, but Cromwell went farther, ready to accept and publish his own face with every blemish distinct. It wasn't in his nature to seek charm or amulet to get rid of them.

Toulouse-Lautrec, in his role of portrait painter, declared, "I have no mercy on warts," which he pointed up and decorated with hairs. He would have liked Cromwell's warts, most of them on his chin (unlike the Miller's on the tip of his nose: "A werte and thereon stood a tuft of heres, / Reed as the bristles of a sowes eres"). After a long look at the Cromwell portrait, I had come to respect the modesty of his character.

But lately in the town of Huntingdon, his birthplace, I visited the Cromwell Museum, full of his portraits both with and without warts. I must say I liked the warty ones better. They seemed, as protuberances, less disfiguring than triumphant, proof of a humble, resolute disposition, "Guided by faith and matchless fortitude," wrote Milton.

An attendant, gratified by my interest in a man who had admitted his imperfections, called out in a shrill voice across the museum: "Oh, Mr. Jenkins! Here's a lady who is keen on Cromwell's warts!"

Two schoolgirls snickered.

"Never mind," I said hastily. But Mr. Jenkins hurried forward.

"Well now, it's true, isn't it? He did *have* the warts, didn't he?" he said, an ingratiating man. "You can't so much blame him, I mean, it can happen after a person reaches a certain age."

I told him I genuinely admired the warts. I said I had made a pilgrimage to see them and in embarrassment bent my head to study Cromwell's signature on the official documents exhibited in the glass cases. By the 1650's, I noticed with a pang of regret, he had stopped signing himself plain Oliver Cromwell. He now appeared with a distinct flourish as Oliver P (for Protector). Cromwell had refused the crown in 1657 when it was offered him. But he had accepted the title of Protector as substitute for King, and his accession was proclaimed by her. 's with regal ceremony.

For a modest man and Puritan, I had to admit, it gave him too imperious an air, too royal a look.

Yet Cromwell said once in debate: "I beseech you to think it possible you may be wrong."

Oliver's Warts

Were I at heart an art collector,
Over the mantel, over the bed,
I'd hang a view of the Lord Protector,
Oliver Cromwell's noble head.

Then every wart for extra measure
On Oliver's face would be a sight
Affording pause, reflection, pleasure,
Morning, afternoon, and night.

A smooth Venetian brow or Flemish
Chin is possibly more fair,
But I prefer a modest blemish.
As Oliver said, the warts were there

And to deny a fact, make fainter
Truth, were then a deeper flaw.
Oliver told the portrait painter
To put in everything he saw.

A masterwork to give me knowledge
And offer hope of honest men
I'd buy from Sidney Sussex College
To witness Oliver's warts again.

Mr. Katsimbalis

I sat in Zonar's, having lunch by the front window. The most famous bar in Athens stretched its length down the restaurant. Squeezed in beside me at the next table, three voluble Greeks talked at once. They sounded avant-garde even in Greek. One, louder, fatter, and older than the rest, with a belly like Falstaff's and the voice of a bull, was a roaring raconteur and monologist. His remarks were torrential, unceasing, obviously brilliant.

As I ordered the stuffed cabbage leaves, with Pfaff beer, the heroic talker turned in midsentence. Shifting to excellent English, he leaned over and in an undertone that blew in my ears recommended the chicken-rice dish, of which he was eating his second heaping plate with a bottle of red wine. As gourmet, he said, he could speak poems for the fare at Zonar's.

When his two companions finished and left, the man turned squarely around to face me. He smiled, for a fleeting space silent. Since a briefcase rested beside his chair, I made a quick guess and asked, "Professor?"

"No! Scholar!" roared Georges Katsimbalis, presenting his card. It was the hero of Henry Miller's book on Greece, *The Colossus of Maroussi*. It was the Colossus himself.

Professor was the one thing he was not. For the next hour of uninterrupted monologue, he outlined with a waving of hands like an impresario the history of his life and talents for the last millennium or so as scholar, poet, translator, wit, bibliographer, critic, editor of a literary review, linguist, traveler, authority on Greece, bon vivant, connoisseur of wine and women, gossip, teller of fabulous lies. And egoist. He kept going full tilt, stabbing the air with digressions and dilations.

Henry Miller met him thirty-five years ago on a visit to Greece. Miller said then, "I listened spellbound, enchanted by every phrase he let drop. I saw that he was made for the monologue. . . . The man could galvanize the dead with his talk. . . . It wasn't just talk he handed out, but *language*—"

What a meeting that was, colossus with colossus. "He seemed to be talking about himself all the time," Miller said, without trying in his book to reproduce the talk. One fascinating story Katsimbalis had told haunted him for days, though "like all his stories, I find it impossible to transcribe." Its haunting nature we must take on faith; in any case, Katsimbalis fell asleep halfway through, took a long nap, and never finished. "He talked about himself because he himself was the most interesting person he knew. I liked that quality very much—I have a little of it myself." A little? They both reeled with it, inebriate of self.

Lawrence Durrell, who knew Katsimbalis well, had introduced them. In writing about his old friend to Miller in the spring of 1940, Durrell referred in wonder to that "Wagnerian cycle of stories." "Pouring drink into him," said Durrell, "is like pouring nitroglycerine into a safe."

How could Miller do him justice? In *The Colossus of Maroussi* (the most praised of his books, Miller's favorite), the Colossus is drowned out, his voice inaudible above Miller's own. A man is talking, talking, but it is the author who raves and bellows, lost in his own inexhaustible reveries, egocentric, deaf. He assumes the rapt attitude of listener and hears one extraordinary blast of sound, a man listening to himself.

At the end of the book, Miller asks forgiveness of Katsimbalis for having exaggerated him into a Colossus. He de-

nies there is anything grandiose after all about Katsimbalis
or about Maroussi (the suburb of Athens where he lived).
Miller adds, "Neither, in the ultimate, is there anything
grandiose about the entire history of Greece." That takes
care of that, neatly disposing of everything classical since
Homer ("I've never read a line of Homer," says Miller).

I enjoyed meeting Mr. Katsimbalis. You don't run into
a colossus every day, and I too listened spellbound as to
a stream relentlessly flowing, unable afterward to recall
what he said—except that Miller's book had made him infamous, the butt of ridicule in Athens. Yet he said it with
pride and satisfaction; afterward he had paid a happy visit
to Miller at Big Sur. When a halt came to the eloquence
with the end of the red wine, I spoke up.

"What is your opinion of poetry today, Mr. Katsimbalis?"

There was an opening all right. His reply was prompt but
his breath was gone; the interview was over. It became a
curtain speech, suitably terse, immoderate and memorable.

"All Greeks are poets," said Mr. Katsimbalis, shaking
my hand. "I am a Greek myself."

Next day at Zonar's, the man at the adjoining table
looked to be a tragic lyric poet of fifty, one who spoke in
panegyrics, paeans, and dithyrambs. He was courting a
girl of twenty in dark glasses, and the affair was going
badly. He declaimed with energy what sounded like a
choral ode in Greek hexameters, then with an elegant gesture that knocked over his wine glass burst into English.

"I love you!" he said. "I need you psychologically."

"Speak in whispers," she murmured, mopping up the
tablecloth.

"In whispers? Speak in WHISPERS? Am I a whispering

poet?" He lowered his voice to a shout. "I love you! I need you! I want you!"

They left hurriedly.

I sat there eavesdropping, wishing I were Greek, wishing I had two languages to declare my affections in.

"To have seen Athens gives a man what Swift calls Invisible Precedence over his fellows."

—Edward Marsh, *A Number of People*

On the Acropolis white daisies bloomed in February. A storm threatened, though streaks of sunlight crisscrossed Athens to the Aegean. No one walked on the heights. At the summit, the roofless Parthenon had turned golden in the halflight. Still there in the center of her temple stood blue-eyed Athene, goddess of wisdom, her flesh of purest ivory, her raiment of pure gold. The forty-foot goddess made by Phidias, a lady missing for centuries, still rose to dominate her holy place, the *parthenon* (temple of the maiden). When the sun caught the gold of Athene, she blinded the eyes. To see her was to forget the world.

A man's head appeared above the broken steps of the Parthenon. He gave a quick look round and turned impatient to the woman behind him. "But the place is empty, empty!" he said. "There's absolutely nothing in it. What is it *for*, anyway? What did they *do* here?"

In the Parthenon Room at the British Museum, where England has held on to the Elgin marbles since 1803, you see some peculiar sights—a statue of Athene consisting only of her breasts (the rest of her stayed behind in Athens). Bernard Berenson, like Plato, said that when a statue is truly beautiful you never miss the head. Actually I do. I like the body intact: head, face, torso, extremities, all. It might be a good idea to collect Athene one day and reassemble her.

Niki and the Four-Day Classical Tour

The Four-Day Classical Tour sets out from Athens at 8:00 A.M. on Wednesday during the winter season and returns on Saturday night. Shorter tours leave daily for Delphi and the Peloponnesus, unless snow makes mountain roads impassable. Only this tour is called "classical," in words printed large across the side of the huge comfortable bus.

Though it seated forty, we were fourteen passengers on a sunny morning in February, plus the Greek driver and a woman guide. The others were in their seats when B. and I climbed aboard, the last to be picked up at our hotel, the Alexiou. I stared at them, since they would be our close companions for the rest of the week. Four recognized us and smiled; we had met before. The two spinsters up front were on the plane to Crete last Saturday—two sisters, retired schoolteachers from Milwaukee. Gordon and Judy Ley from Maryland we had met three days ago in Heraklion. They were about forty and good company. I was happy to see them again.

That made six Americans. By listening to the buzz of talk, I picked out three more: a white-haired stout woman from Colorado, a dark-haired thin one from Hawaii, a pretty girl from Texas. But the bus was about to start. The guide rose from her seat beside the driver.

"Good morning," she said with a warm smile. Oh, I liked her! *"Est-ce qu'il y a personne ici qui parle français?"*

"Ah oui, madame," called a young man from the rear. The little redhead beside him echoed, *"Ah oui."*

"I understood this tour was to be conducted in English!"

barked a middle-aged man opposite us. By his accent he was German. By her look so was his heavy-faced wife.

"That it will be," the guide answered. "I said good morning, didn't I? We shall speak French for the French visitors. I'm sorry, sir, my German is not good enough."

Without deigning to reply, he opened his guidebook— a grumpy man if not rude. Would he be the complainer, already making a fuss?

Nine Americans then, a French couple, a German couple, two Greeks to convey us. And the fourteenth passenger? In flowered kerchief and glasses, she might be an American graduate student, a plain earnest type with a nervous giggle. As our guide pursued the question of language, she revealed herself: a German medical doctor, who spoke all four languages represented in the bus and didn't mind which she listened to. I studied her with respectful attention. If we fell ill on this journey or were at a loss for words she would prove useful. She was an old hand at classical tours, having twice taken this one. She modestly reminded the guide they had met before.

The guide introduced herself: Niki, meaning "victory" like Athene Nike on the Acropolis. Most Greeks are named for gods or goddesses, unless they're called George. Niki looked past thirty, a short, sturdy, black-haired, forthright woman, whose face lit up as she spoke. No wedding ring was on her finger. She seemed not tense but intense, her voice low-pitched but positive. She spoke English with a marked accent, less fluently than French. She plunged into her work—"We have a far way to go"—blowing into her microphone to test it and began, as if every word would open a door.

"In ancient Greece were the five great shrines: Delphi and Delos, shrines of Apollo. Olympia, dedicated to Zeus and the Olympic games. Epidaurus, hospital for the body. Eleusis, healing place of the soul."

Niki repeated this in French, while we gazed out the window. We were traveling the Sacred Way between Athens and Eleusis, where the pilgrims went on foot to learn the mysteries of life and death. We were tourists (deprived of the joy of Knowing), not pilgrims. At 8:30 A.M., we stopped at Daphni, six miles from Athens, at an eleventh-century Byzantine church on the site of a temple of Apollo.

In the paved courtyard, Niki plucked a green sprig from a tree. "Laurel," she said, "*le laurier*. Daphni is Greek for laurel, sacred to Apollo. She was a girl loved by the god, you remember, changed into such a small tree."

The little yellow church was bare and empty, save for what remained of its splendid gold mosaics. We gathered close to Niki under the cupola, where the stern bearded Christ Pantocrator, pale and terrible in his majesty, frowned grief-stricken on this world with black piercing eyes.

Niki pointed smiling at the walls, as if she hadn't seen them before, the jewel-like mosaics of the Annunciation, Nativity, Baptism, Crucifixion, searching our faces to find if we shared her delight, while the gold of the radiant church made the shadows appear sunlit. The German couple had wandered away, paying her no heed.

Three cats played under the cypresses as we left. "In Greece," Niki was saying. "everyone is orthodox. There is but the one church, the Christian God. We are not allowed to say, 'I am nothing.'"

The handsome young driver, Lambros, handed us into the bus, then swung around to take the toll road to Corinth. We would cross Attica to the Corinth Canal, which connects the Aegean with the Ionian Sea and gave us entrance to the Peloponnesus. Beyond Megara we reached the dramatic canal, where all but the German couple chose to walk the seventy-five feet across the high steel bridge. In his day the emperor Nero tried and failed to build this canal through solid rock, after wielding a golden shovel at the opening ceremony. Ships had to be dragged by land, three miles at the narrowest point, from one sea to the other. Nineteen centuries after Nero, we straggled across the thin cut, its sheer perpendicular sides gashed through rock to the ribbon of water below.

Since our tour, presumably our thoughts, were entirely classical, we hurried through modern Corinth with its Hotel Byron and drove five miles to the hill site of the ancient city. Scattered ruins were dominated by the seven remaining pillars of the Temple of Apollo. Corinth's greatness came in the sixth century B.C. Wiped out by the Roman Mummius, rebuilt under Julius Caesar into stately temples and gardens, what we saw flattened in ruin was mostly Roman.

Niki, pure Greek, showed precious little respect for latecomers like the invaders from Rome. "Corinth was a splendid Greek city, her patron saint the goddess Aphrodite," she said firmly. Never call her Venus. The Temple of Aphrodite once rose on the Acrocorinth, where a thousand courtesans came in her honor to offer to the devout their pious but fleshly wares. They celebrated a festival called Aphrodisia.

"Follow me," said Niki, and led us to the Pirene spring, where the winged horse Pegasus came to drink. It was another favorite meeting place of the prostitutes, who wore gold sandals printed with the words "Follow me" and the price clearly marked. The high cost of love gave rise to the proverb "Not every man can journey to Corinth." Theirs was a thriving holy profession.

The courtesan Laïs (to whom Aphrodite appeared in a dream as a mark of favor) grew so celebrated throughout Greece that when Demosthenes sought her he found her price (according to Lemprière, whose *Classical Dictionary* I carried under my arm) about £300 in English money. The orator departed, saying he wouldn't buy repentance at so dear a price. Yet Diogenes the cynic, filthy and penniless, enjoyed her favors free—Diogenes who preached the doctrine of virtuous self-control.

"The Pirene spring, being immortal, is never dry," Niki said, but I didn't taste this clear flowing water. Who knows what sweet erotic nectar it might be, how disastrous the effect?

Small wonder that St. Paul stood in the marketplace of Corinth in A.D. 51 and preached for the next year to the corrupt, flesh-loving Corinthians: "This love of which I speak—" One could still hear him, it seemed, and hear the echoing voice of Keats's Corinthian youth, Lycius, "heart-struck and lost," destroyed by evil and destroyed by love.

Mycenae lies between two grim, stony mountains in Argolis. They say a light on one of them announced the victory of Troy. Here Agamemnon, King of Men, ruler of the powerful kingdom of Mycenae, passed through this Lion Gate when he left for Troy, reentering it on his triumphant return ten years later (1184 B.C., the usual date), only to be murdered that night by his wife Clytemnestra and her lover Aegisthus.

She struck him twice, says Aeschylus, twice he cried out, "Alas, I have been struck deep a mortal wound." With her axe she gave a third and final blow. For this death Orestes the avenger killed his mother, then fled the kingdom pursued by the Furies. Only Homer and the tragic poets had told the fearful story of Mycenae, that is, till Schliemann came in 1876 and told it again.

Schliemann dug to uncover what lies revealed beyond the Lion Gate (its two stone headless lionesses ten feet high)—the fortress of Mycenae itself. There he found the circle of royal graves, six shaft tombs with their nineteen skeletons: nine men, eight women, two babies wrapped in gold. And he rejoiced to believe, mistakenly, he had beheld the body of Agamemnon, the crumbling face hidden by a thin gold mask. "Today I have looked on the face of Agamemnon. . . . "

"Golden Mycenae," Homer called it. Schliemann found plenty of gold in the graves, for Mycenae was late Minoan, a last stage of that great civilization risen from Crete. Like the palaces of Knossos and Phaestos, it had a time of gold magnificence, then it fell, disappearing from the sight or memory of men.

An avenue of eucalyptus trees led to the citadel from the broad plain of Argolis. We had ridden as far as Lambros could take us. After our lunch in the modern town of Mycenae, we were refreshed and ready for the tombs: shaft tombs, chamber tombs, beehive tombs. We had a fine appetite for tombs. Outside the Lion Gate, Niki pointed to the so-called tombs of Clytemnestra and Aegisthus (buried beyond the walls, wrote Pausanias, because unworthy to lie beside Agamemnon and Cassandra). Our retired Milwaukee schoolteachers interrupted eagerly to relate the bloody tragedy—to the complete bewilderment of most of the listeners.

"But if they *weren't* buried here, what's the point of the story? Who *was* buried here anyway?"

Niki laughed. "Who knows? They came and went long ago, long before the Trojan War. Men of peace, perhaps?"

Silently, in the deathlike silence, we filed through the

Lion Gate, stepping in ruts worn by ancient chariot wheels.
Not a soul was about in February. Inside on the windy
ridge, a few shattered walls of Mycenae remained, beside
them a ring of stark upright slabs encircling the open
graves, the six empty tombs.

I was frightened. It seemed an unbearable place, barbaric, appalling, full of menace and desolation, cursed by
the gods and drenched in blood. Thirty centuries ago it had
been destroyed by some awful conflagration, abandoned
to the dead to be forgotten. Yet here we were, like Pausanias of old, poking among the ruins.

The bleak path kept straight to the summit of the mountain, where along this slope the palace once stood, now rubble partly fallen into the ravine. Niki stopped talking, her
eyes fixed in dismay. "Look!" she cried, staring at our
German Herr, who had disappeared an hour ago, bobbing
up on the very top of the mountain. No telling where his
Frau had got to. We could see his gray head high on the
ramparts as he ignored our shouts. Since we couldn't get
him down or, as Gordon suggested, leave him behind, I
seized the moment to climb up too in a furious wind for the
sight of this evil-haunted Mycenae, and far below the empty
plain of Argolis.

Patiently Niki collected us and led us down the hill to
another excavation, the great beehive tomb of the House of
Atreus. Was it here Agamemnon was in fact buried, the
son of Atreus laid to rest among his royal ancestors? A
road cut into the mountainside and lined with stone led to
the massive doorway of stone blocks. Within was a dark
vault forty feet high, empty of the bodies once placed on
the rocky floor, plundered of its jewels. Niki touched the
blackened wall beside which shepherds must have lit fires
centuries ago in an abandoned tomb.

Back in our bus where Lambros waited, we drove

through Argos on the plain with its pistachio trees and miles of lemon groves. I asked Niki to show me Tiryns, and nine miles farther she had the bus slowed to a crawl. Little was left of the walled city beside the Aegean where a Minoan palace stood even older than Mycenae. No sign remained of the happy people of Tiryns (Niki knew the story from Athenaeus, but she didn't unsettle the group by telling it)—who were so irrepressibly merry, full of unquenchable laughter, that in shame they went to the oracle at Delphi to ask Apollo how to become sober and restrained.

Apollo answered they must sacrifice a bull to Poseidon by casting it into the sea without a smile. To undertake this painful task, the people of Tiryns shut out, as too playful, all children from the ceremony. But as they were about to throw the bull, a little boy slipped into the group and cried, "What's the matter? Are you afraid I will upset your victim?" At that the populace burst into roars of laughter. So they were punished, left as they were, the merriest of Greeks, to which they resigned themselves and, guilty of laughter, went on laughing.

By the time we reached Epidaurus, in the Argive mountains, the afternoon grew late. Niki had talked steadily all day in three languages, yet appeared obsessed to say more. The little French couple, who must be on their honeymoon, had listened in awe when their turn came, holding tight to each other.

The plump little wife looked eighteen, with bright auburn hair, turned-up nose, round blue eyes, and freckles—even on her knees, I noticed at lunch. The husband was her height but older, with a shrewd face and black hair. They wore new navy-blue raincoats exactly alike, and, possessive in love, he handed her over the stony paths as if she would break. Judy believed she might be pregnant, but I thought not necessarily.

Though there were sixty-three shrines of Aesculapius (in Greek Asclepius, god of health, son of Apollo by a mortal woman), this main shrine at Epidaurus had brought the sick from near and far. Pilgrims came by boat from Athens, stayed a month among the temples and baths, and gave thanks to the god who restored them.

"They came to him with ulcers the flesh had grown," wrote Pindar, "their limbs mangled and bruised, their bodies stormed with fever or chill. And he released each man and led him from his individual grief."

Afterward they would present to the god a replica of the hurt part—a marble hand, leg, ear, a stone baby, a terra-cotta model of affliction: an ulcered breast, a withered arm, a gouty toe, a blinded eye, a sterile penis, a stricken brain. Niki read us votive tablets of miraculous cures by the healer Asclepius, who came to the ailing in a dream. By their own faith he cured them. Yet Pindar says Asclepius was killed by a thunderbolt from Zeus when he presumed to bring a dead man back to life.

A barren woman once asked that she might conceive a child.

"Is that all you want?" Asclepius inquired.

"That is all."

She became pregnant and stayed so for five years. Tired of waiting, she returned to Epidaurus and requested she might also bear the child. The wish was instantly granted. The child, a five-year-old boy, ran off at birth and bathed in the fountain. Asclepius liked people to be exact in the language of their beseeching.

While I listened, I thought of the last words of dying Socrates as the hemlock crept upwards in his body. "Crito,

I owe a cock to Asclepius," he said, whatever he meant by that.

"The debt shall be paid," said Crito. "Is there anything else?" There was no answer.

A cock, sacred to the god, was the usual offering of sacrifice. Did Socrates, accused at his trial of neglect of the gods, owe a debt too late? Or was death itself the final cure?

We sat now in the immense theater, in front-row seats reserved for royalty, and gazed up at the semicircle like a huge fan carved out of the hillside. The indefatigable Niki struck a match from the center of the stage. "Can you hear it?" Perfectly, we laughed, only twenty feet away. Here was the real miracle of Epidaurus, where once a year the great tragedies used to be performed. Yet how lonely a ruined theater seemed at twilight. That latter-day traveler in Greece Henry Miller said he found here "the morning of the first day of the great peace, the peace of the heart"—something like that. In our time could Epidaurus effect a cure? Was it still the healing place of the heart?

The eighteen miles to Nauplia grew heavy with traffic —fifty sheep and their shepherd, a dozen donkeys in file laden with olive branches. Then the Amphitryon Hotel rose on the seafront, and suddenly I wanted to give up the Classical Tour to live forever with a room and balcony overlooking the Aegean.

At Nauplia the goddess Hera used to bathe in a fountain yearly to renew her virginity, a pretty custom for the wife of Zeus. Tonight the roar of wind and sea where Sophocles on the Aegean heard it long ago was only the plaintive sound of a moored craft rocking in the waves, not the ebb and flow of human misery.

Over a reviving bottle of golden retsina, we sat with Gordon and Judy at dinner, talking exclusively of the U.S.A. To mention the glory of Greece would have been too exhausting.

THE SECOND DAY. 8:00 A.M. As we boarded the tour bus, the faces looked welcoming, all but two smiling. We were congenial, at ease. Niki said into the microphone, "Good morning, my children." She was right, we were children, asking at every hand, "Niki, what do I do?" "Niki, where do I go?" She became strong as we weakened, dedicated in her desire to look after us. We trusted her judgment, accepted her word; she asked in return only our love of Greece.

"On a tour, sometimes it is complaints from everybody." (One aggrieved old lady had said, "You haven't told us where you raise spaghetti.") "But not from good children like you. From you, no fretting at all." The German Herr scowled.

She hated to forget an English word or mispronounce one. B. usually knew what she meant and supplied it, "the professor," she called him. Niki said *shell* for *shield*, *bottle* for *battle*. If she accepted help with her English, she wanted none whatever with her subject. "No, no, no, no, NO!" she cried in a fury if contradicted. Her professional pride was intense.

We began to climb rock-strewn mountains, still in Argolis. What madness led tourists to have themselves hauled up these peaks, only to be dashed headlong down again? "Greece is nothing but mountains," sighed B., "one damned summit after another." Just then we descended pellmell, the road shone in the sun, a rainbow bent over us. We entered Arcadia.

And Arcadia was *nothing* but mountains! The poets sang
—didn't they?—of a pastoral landscape with gentle slopes,
where shepherds strolled under the trees and Pan chased
the nymphs and hamadryads. But were Virgil and Milton
ever *in* Arcadia? (Apparently Ovid was, since he pictured
a savage place fit for beasts.) Here the steep rocks and
crags explained why Pan had the hairy legs of a goat.
Among these precipices, one looked in vain for a single wood
nymph, a single Arcadian shepherd feeding on acorns. We
passed an ordinary man riding sideways on a donkey, and
we crawled up, up, up, above the highest mountainside
where cherry trees were in bloom. "Come, for we call you,
shepherd, from the hills."

Tripolis, chief town of Arcadia, was no more Arcadian
than I am, a busy Greek city three thousand feet above the
sea. Wine and silkworms came from Tripolis, hardly the
concern of simple shepherds. Yet it was unforgettable for
good reason—for one word written in white stones against
the mountain, each stark letter visible for miles. Oχι, the
word was, No. The Greeks said "NO!" to the Turks during
the Occupation; they said it again in defiance of the Germans. No, never.

Cloud-capped we ascended. Like Poussin, I, too, had
lived in Arcadia—for three solid hours—in a scene more
precipitous and vertical than Poussin had in mind. My fear
was only Panic (the kind felt by travelers in Arcadia), a
groundless, irrational terror attributable to the great god
Pan.

We stopped for refreshment at a perched village four
thousand feet up, Vytina, noted for its yoghurt, a delicacy
not everyone fancied. But Niki did and I did. Carol from
Colorado took two helpings of the creamy curds and honey.
She was, she told us, a writer of cookbooks and articles

for *Gourmet*. "A gourmet!" exclaimed Niki, as if that was all we needed. Carol's eyes glowed as she explained how to boil an artichoke or braise an endive. She had once eaten a meal in Paris cooked by Alice B. Toklas. "I'm on my way around the world," she said, "to gather material for a new book, *Around the World in Eighty Dishes*. One dish, of course, will be Greek." I was impressed by Carol's methods of research. To choose a four-day classical tour seemed a hightoned way to go about it.

The heady perfume came from nearby fir forests. I wanted to take home a baby cypress ("Yon cypress that points like death's lean lifted forefinger"). Instead Judy and I strolled across the marketplace to inspect the wares of Phidias and Praxiteles, two woodcarvers of Vytina, where we bought a necklace apiece of hand-carved wooden beads and in the bus found the two retired schoolteachers decked out in the same.

As Lambros raced down the perpendicular mountain, the silence grew acute while we held our breath. "Surprise!" shouted Niki. "I promised you a surprise." Were we descending our last Arcadian mountain to a nice flat plain? Oh no. She leaned out the window to point to a village clinging to the steep slope: "Langadia, the most beautiful town in Greece and in the world. It is Eden, the Promised Land. Only happy people live in Langadia." Isolated towns like this were built during the Occupation in fear of the Turks. This one hung like a pendant jewel.

Et in Arcadia ego. We left it to enter the district of Ellis at its feet, and my heart rose up in the valley and I stared entranced at the river Alpheus, near which Pan tried to seduce that chaste girl Syrinx. Syrinx was a virgin whose chastity so went to her head she dressed like Diana. When Pan, who had marked success in making love to

nymphs, lusted after her, she said No and fled, appealing
to the gods as she ran. At last he caught the winded girl
beside the river Ladon (a tributary of the Alpheus), held
her in a hot embrace, and found he clutched a bunch of
reeds to his breast.

The best part comes next. Pan sighed in honest regret
and the reeds sighed also ("Poor nymph, poor Pan," sighed
Keats in his poem). What a pity. But hearing the soft mel-
ody the reeds made, Pan quickly took up seven of them
and fashioned a flute, a Pan pipe, a Syrinx. As he played
he murmured with sensible pleasure: *This much I have!*

Though we had traveled toward it all morning, Olympia
appeared without warning on the level plain. Beside the
road lay the Stadium, little more than a large mowed
field with embankments and a clearly marked starting
point and finishing line.

At the Hotel Spap, six little Greek maids ran twittering
to meet us, take our luggage to our rooms, and serve us
lunch with trembling hands. We walked forth with Niki,
across the hotel terrace to the ruins a few yards away, and
having nowhere else to go wandered about all afternoon.

Olympia was always a sanctuary, never a town. Now
it looked a wooded park full of pines, strangely littered
with broken pillars and stone rubble, the grass carpeted
with blue iris and crimson anemones (sprung from the
blood of Adonis). At the sight we women stooped to pick
bouquets, ignoring the ruins of the Gymnasium, while Niki
talked on tirelessly as she hopped from flower to flower.
The German doctor knelt and took a snapshot of an iris.
Olympia was serene in the sun filtering through the trees,
a place of peace. It had Olympian calm.

Following the anemones we moved toward the Temple

of Zeus, in whose honor the sacred games were held. The
Herr, unaccountably among us, glanced up in annoyance
from his guidebook and directed his first question of the
tour to Niki. She jumped, startled.

"Inform me, please, why there is a Temple of Olympian
Zeus in Athens and a Temple of Olympian Zeus here. Why
two?"

"Why not?"

"I wish to know why. Isn't *this* Olympia?"

"Zeus was the god of Mt. Olympus."

He walked off in a huff and listened no more.

The Temple of Zeus stood for eight hundred years, within it the statue of the god, one of the Seven Wonders of
the World—so magnificent some took it for Zeus himself.
Phidias made it not from a living model but by asking himself what form a god would take if he chose to become
visible. To die without beholding him was considered ill
fate; to see him one forgot all sorrow. He was seated on a
gold throne, a king forty feet high of ivory and gold, precious gems imbedded in his beard and hair, his eyes two
gleaming jewels, his robe and sandals of gold, his mantle
embroidered with white lilies and green leaves, his feet
resting on a golden footstool. Strabo said, "If it should
rise and stand upright, it would unroof the temple."

Niki led us to Phidias' workshop where he created this
Zeus. The immortal work had ended, like everything else,
in oblivion. Like all gods, Zeus was insecure on his throne.
Theodosius (having stopped the Olympic games) destroyed
the Temple in A.D. 426 to make room for a Christian god;
he built a Byzantine church over the workshop of Phidias.
But Zeus hurled the last thunderbolt at his desecrated
shrine, when it fell in storm and earthquake and the ruined
columns crashed to the ground.

The Olympic games lasted a thousand years. Admission was free to free males of Greece, with wars suspended for the interval. No slave and no woman might attend, under penalty of death. A woman of Rhodes, Callipatira, slipped in disguised as a trainer, but when her son was declared victor she leaped for joy and exposed her person. Though her life was mercifully spared as mother, sister, daughter of athletes, after that even the trainers had to go naked. The youths ran, jumped, wrestled, boxed, threw discus and javelin (five events in one day) clad only in olive oil and a layer of dust to keep from slipping. The reward was a crown of wild olives, with no second prize—to be second was to fail. Since the winner had proved himself a man and a hero, what more did he want? (If he wanted more, he might set up his statue at Olympia, no larger than life-size.)

There were chariot races and poetry contests. Nero fell off his chariot twice, abandoned the race, won first prize. Herodotus read history at Olympia, Pindar recited his odes and victory-songs: "Zeus Accomplisher, grant them modesty," Socrates talked, Plato taught. Professor Kitto (in *The Greeks*) tells of Diogenes, who saw young men from Rhodes bedecked in fine robes and exclaimed, "Affectation!" The next moment catching sight of some grubby Spartans, ill-kempt and shabby, he cried, "More affectation!"

We women picked the shriveled olives clinging to the sacred trees and walked free at Olympia, marching behind Niki like athletes (with our clothes on) down the Sacred Way to the Stadium. Three men—Gordon, B., the French husband—accompanied us; we had lost the Herr. The Alpheus flowed silent. Black-and-white magpies flew across the sky.

We reached the starting line and stood ranged along it (with room for twenty runners), placing our toes in the triangular grooves. Gordon and I crouched side by side on the mark, set off down the field in a puffing little foot race. The sprint was two hundred yards to the finish line, but we bogged down in mud and the event was inconclusive. I wasn't the first woman to race at Olympia, since a few girl runners preceded me ages before. Suddenly in the midst of our foolery came a crashing downpour of rain. This time we really ran, blinded and sopping wet, fleeing back to the hotel. Ahead of me Niki, a fast runner, stopped dead.

"Wait!" she yelled. "*Stop!* This you must see, the Temple of Hera." The rain splashed down her eager face as the others raced past her, too drowned to care. "Wait, *arrêtez!* The Hermes of Praxiteles, it was found here." Halted behind her, I gazed respectfully at the two remaining pillars, holding up my bunch of wilting anemones. The spring flood would do them good.

After dinner that night Niki was white with fatigue, so exhausted the English words refused to come. She opened her mouth—no sound. Yet she paused at our coffee table to make sure we were well fed, happy.

"O, Niki, Niki, I love Greece!" I burst out, startling myself. "In two short days you have taught me why." She laughed, and her eyes filled with tears. She bent down and kissed my cheek.

In bed I lay awake counting the riches—Phidias' delicate implements (in the museum at Olympia), his cup engraved "This cup belongs to Phidias." Niki forever urged us to imagine these things not in museums but back where they belonged, like the helmet of Miltiades found with his name on it in the Stadium. Before I fell asleep, I lifted up

a statue of pure white Parian marble, the Hermes of Praxiteles, and carried it in the rain back to its pedestal in the
Temple of Hera. Hermes, the fleetest runner, Hermes, the
god of travelers. They say one can see three changing ex-
pressions on his lovely face—dreamy, pensive, and today,
I thought, quizzical, standing awkwardly as he did in a box
of sand to keep from toppling to harm.

THE THIRD DAY. 8:00 A.M. We had become friends, a
talkative, congenial company. I knew something about
everybody. The dark-haired sweet-faced woman traveling
with Carol the gourmet was an artist from Hawaii. She
took notes on Greek vases. Carol called her Zohmah.

The German doctor's name was Rosemarie. This morning she had exclaimed "My *God*ness!" as the sun came
out. Did she mean the goodness of God? Or the godness of
Greece?

The shy bachelor girl, Helen, who sat with Rosemarie in
the bus, hailed from Texas and worked at Stuttgart in a
USAF hospital. Her manner was timid, her voice faint. Up
to now we had exchanged a few endorsing adjectives at the
ruins.

And the German Frau? She wore a tall beaver hat like
Chaucer's Merchant and occupied herself by looping a
brown scarf over the top, tying it under her chin. Dull, im-
passive, she blinked in surprise and turned away if one
smiled at her. She gave no sign of understanding English,
or German either when her husband read aloud from his
guidebook. They ate alone, walked alone, fended for themselves, sharing fruit and digestive pills. I think they weren't
hostile but coldly indifferent. They had no habit of friendli-
ness with strangers.

Niki looked rested this morning. "Such charming children," she began. "What will you ask today? Niki, what

flower is this? Niki, what time is lunch?" Calla lilies bloomed in the dooryards of Pyrgos. In the distance lay the gray Ionian Sea. The French couple had moved their seats closer to the group. Now directly in front of us, the French wife kissed her husband a hot smack. His face glowed at this giving way to passion.

By the third day of wandering over the Peloponnesus, we had lost track of time. From his seat behind us, Gordon guessed the date to be February 21, and I hunted up a calendar in my purse to see. If today was in fact Friday, it must be the 22nd, what we used to call George Washington's birthday. Gordon was still skeptical.

On the shining road to Aegion beside the Bay of Patras, Niki abruptly halted the bus. Yesterday I had said, "Niki, will you show me some asphodel?" and now Lambros jumped out to pick two tall stalks of the pale-pink flowers. As Niki brought them down the aisle, the German wife reached out her hand. "No, I'm sorry," said Niki sharply, handing me the flowers. "Take them to America, my dear, to show your schoolchildren." Since there were two spikes of asphodel, the Frau was welcome to one of them. She took it without a word and left it on the windowsill to wilt and die.

From Aegion, the ferry crossed the Gulf of Corinth in three hours. After picking up our box lunch, already waiting in pink paper bags at the Aegion café, whose sign said "*Pour les fins gourmets*," we were free for twenty minutes before the ferry left. I bought a jar of rose petal jam (not that I like it; it was the speciality of the town), then walked over to lean against an aged, gnarled plane tree in the square. A placard on the trunk said "Pausanias' plane tree." Pausanias passed through Aegion around A.D. 200, in the time of Marcus Aurelius.

"Our ferry is the *Thalia*," Niki said as we climbed

aboard the bus. "Three ancient ferryboats make this cross-ing to Itea, and all of them are bad. This one is the worst."

Carol groaned. She suggested a bottle of wine for solace, and after consultation Niki bought an expensive one for her in the café. At 12:15 we drove onto the ferry—a battered landing craft from World War II—went to the dining saloon, ate our gourmet sandwiches with beer bought on the boat, talked, and all at once realized we had never left the dock. *Where was Niki?* What on earth had happened? We looked at each other in consternation. Something had gone wrong.

With a grand flourish in rushed Niki waving Carol's bottle of wine. Having discovered at the dock the café owner had sold her an inferior brand, she had held up the ferry till the man was notified and came running a half-mile with the right one. That is how Niki took care of her children.

On the upper deck in a blaze of sunshine, we stared ex-pectant toward an invisible Parnassus. Water and sky were the same sapphire blue. Judy leaned on the rail beside me and confided she was a descendant of Anne Bradstreet.

"You may not have heard of her," Judy added, "but she was a kind of poet. I've inherited a desk supposed to have been hers."

"Not *heard* of her?" I cried. And we laughed, because we were Americans and this was George Washington's birthday.

The French husband, standing on my right, revealed a modest knowledge of English. "Regard the caves there," he said, pointing to the shore. "*Alors*, one may imagine mer-maids." He was with Air France in Paris. His little wife snuggled close, proud of his eloquence.

As we approached the port of Itea, Niki came to tell us what we were solemnly gazing at: Mt. Parnassus in sunlight and shadow, a sheer height of bare rock. Now Delphi appeared, suspended in a cleft of the rock, a cluster of white houses perched on a shelf on the mountainside. I trembled at the perpendicular climb to reach there. Yet this was the way the pilgrims came. They had climbed on foot straight up to Delphi, perhaps like me with anxiety in their hearts.

The dock at Itea was covered with a hundred barrels of Greek olives (though the crop had been reaped in November), each barrel labeled in English from "small" to "extra jumbo"—the first time I've known an olive admitted to be small. They should have said "sacred," coming ripe and holy from the groves of the god Apollo.

Through a lane of eucalyptus we drove toward Parnassus, emerging into a world of olive trees filling the plain. "Fifteen miles of olives," said Niki, "a *million* olive trees." They thrived on hard rocky soil, long-lived and vigorous, admirable characters like some people I've known. As we began to climb, we looked back on olive groves—pale-green wall-to-wall carpet from mountain to sea.

Asphodel bloomed on the slopes of Parnassus and pink flowering almond trees. The scene became wilder, barren, fierce, as we climbed straight up over rocks, a busful of sixteen people pretending to be a goat.

"Look, *look!* An eagle, there's an eagle," Niki yelled. One soared over us, then two followed close behind.

That afternoon in a swirling wind we walked from the village to the ruins of Delphi, the top of the world. Why would one mount higher still to the actual summit? (Byron did, on a mule: "Oh, thou Parnassus! whom I now survey.") We were already at the mystery, the abode of the god. The bare cliffs of the Phaedriades hung over us. An eagle hovered and dropped to its nest, then seven more swooped to the sky. Niki waved at them, as pleased as if she had ordered the spectacle.

"For God's sake, don't ask her to show us an elephant," said Carol.

From the semicircle of the theater, with the desolate Temple of Apollo beyond, we peered down the tremendous gorge, then lifted our eyes to Parnassus shadowed in blues and purples in the late-afternoon light. Niki once saw a production of *Medea* in this ruined theater. She heard Medea's screams for her murdered children echoing back horribly from the mountain.

They say the Temple of Apollo was built over a chasm in the rock from which issued vapors of white steam. The temple held a gold statue of Apollo; the walls bore sayings lettered in gold of the Wise Men of Greece—"Know thyself," "Nothing in excess"; and the lovely whore Phryne was there too, the mistress of Praxiteles in solid gold between the statues of the King of Sparta and Philip of Macedon. (Crates the Cynic called it "a votive offering of the profligacy of Greece.") An iron chair was kept for the poet Pindar when he dined with Apollo, conversing I suppose in Doric Greek. In an underground chamber stood the tripod where the priestess, the Pythia, chewing laurel leaves, sat to inhale the vapors and in a frenzy deliver the oracles—"the thunders of Apollo's word," said Euripedes.

"Is there anyone wiser than Socrates?" she was asked. The answer came back straight from the god, "There is no one."

Also in this innermost shrine was a marvelous thing I had come to see (exhibited now in the museum at Delphi): the umbilical stone, the *omphalos*, the belly button of the world. To the Greeks, Delphi marked the exact center of the earth. This stone was its navel.

Who consulted the oracle? Niki loved to talk of that, how for a thousand years they came for advice on war and peace, love and marriage, a journey, a decision, an undertaking. Agamemnon came before leaving for Troy. Rich men like Croesus confidently asked help. Alexander visited Delphi and heard from the priestess, "You are irresistible, my son."

I sat on the steps of the theater listening to Niki, wondering what question I might pose to Apollo were I a man and could. I might ask, "What is the answer?" and hear only, "I wish I knew." No, it was too late. For one thing, the sun god left Delphi for the three months of winter. For a more final reason, the oracle spoke for the last time long ago (to Julian the Apostate). And the Castalia weeps tears.

I alone had the zeal to accompany Niki down the Sacred Way to the Castalian spring. It grew bitter cold and dark. Pliny once counted three thousand statues on this downward path. Hundreds of sparrows flew in and out of the Athenian Treasury (a flight of steps below the Temple of Apollo)—a gift from Athens in gratitude for Marathon. Almond blossoms pelted our faces.

The water of Castalia streamed out of a deep cut from the high Phaedriades, pure water from the holy mountain. It fell into a basin carved of rock and ran down in pools and stone channels to feed the olive groves below.

"Drink it!" said Niki.

The priestess herself would go first to the Castalia, to taste the water of inspiration or bathe in it before prophesying for the oracle. She spoke in verse till there were complaints the god of poetry couldn't be that bad. No doubt the standard was high, with the Nine Muses often residing here as personal friends of Apollo.

Niki and I lay down on our bellies, side by side, and drank long of the nectar. It tasted potent to the tongue, very cold. As we got to our feet, the water of inspiration dripped from my nose and bleared my eyes. This, I think, was the happiest moment of my life.

At the Hotel Delphi, where we spent the night, our room and balcony looked out from a promontory over Parnassus and the Corinthian Gulf. My pale asphodel stood revived in a vase on the bed table. Poets like Homer had made it an immortal flower. The ghosts of the dead walked through meadows of asphodel, forgetful of cares and sorrows.

In the hotel bar before dinner, we nine Americans stood to drink a toast to George Washington. I had ordered a Manhattan with a cherry in it, which struck me as an appropriate and touching tribute.

"Happy birthday, George!" we cried. "First in war, first in peace, first in the hearts of his countrymen."

The German couple observed this ceremony from a table apart in the corner. She blinked her sleepy surprise, but he nodded his head and smiled. It may have been his first smile since Wednesday.

THE FOURTH DAY. I woke early this morning, after dreaming of eagles, and slipped out for a walk before breakfast. I climbed the hill behind the hotel and sat on a rock to enjoy the stupendous view. An eagle and its shadow circled the gorge below. To the left began the village of Delphi, in whose main street strolled a number of black goats.

Down the steep path behind me Rosemarie came striding, a bouquet of anemones in her arms. What an odd name for a German doctor. Should I arise and sing Rudolf Friml's "Rosemarie, I love you"? Instead, I said, "Isn't Niki wonderful?"

Rosemarie sat on a stone beside me. "I tell you, Niki is the most vunderful person I've known in my life."

"How much do you know about her?"

"A little only. She doesn't talk of herself. She is unmarried, no family, nobody. The work is all. It is her life."

"I've learned this, how hard it is to be a good guide. She is really good."

"It's the best career in Greece for a woman," Rosemarie said. "But hard, hard. For years she must study, pass examinations. She must be classical scholar, archaeologist, mythologist, master of two foreign languages. Beyond that, she must have perfect health, liking for people, patience, tact, charm. My *God*ness, most of all endurance."

"Niki has these. And love besides."

"Yes," said Rosemarie. "We are very lucky."

Niki took us to the Delphi museum to help us restore the statues to their original pediments. The first thing I saw at the head of the stairs was the umbilical stone, the navel of the world. It wasn't much to look at, a bit ordinary. Somehow I had expected a round cushion to bounce on or stool to sit on, something shaped like a button. It stood three feet high, a marble block decorated with garlands of wool in relief. Some, like Epimenides of Crete, denied the existence of the *omphalos*. "If any there be," he said, "it is visible to the gods, not visible to mortals." Yet there it was. Buddha should have visited Delphi to contemplate its holy and ponderable navel.

From staring at it, I lost my group. When I joined them Niki was lecturing in French while the French couple gripped each other. She showed them statues of the "Twin Brothers of Argos," Cleobis and Biton, two symmetrical, smiling young men with sturdy naked bodies, each the image of the other. Herodotus gazed at them at Delphi twenty-five centuries ago and told their story: two loving sons who yoked themselves like oxen to a chariot and

pulled their mother six miles to a festival of Hera. In
gratitude for their love, she prayed the goddess to grant
them the highest gift in her power. That night the gift was
given: they died in their sleep.

Niki made careful gestures with her graceful hands, following the lines of a sculpture that appealed to her. She
grew enrapt and would cry, "This I *love!*" or of a Roman
statue or frieze, "I don't *like* it. It's heavy work," and we
passed meekly on. It pleased her if we showed a hint of
intelligence, the least sign of benefit from our four-day
classical education. "What style is this pottery?" Niki
would ask. "Mycenean!" we recited in unison, recognizing
the octupi motifs and the spirals.

In the room where Delphi's great treasure, "The
Charioteer," stood alone, a photographer took pictures. His
lights dazzled. The eyes of the Charioteer gleamed as if
alive, a magnificent young man about nineteen, proud, un-
smiling. His eyes were onyx and ivory (like a line of Yeats,
"All wisdom shut into his onyx eyes"). He had bronze eye-
lashes, lips of red copper, short sculptured hair with a ribbon round his head as a prize for victory. His hands held
the chariot reins; he had just come from the Stadium after
winning the race in 474 B.C. Pausanias saw him long ago
erected near the Temple of Apollo.

We returned to the ruins and plunged down to the Tholos
below the Castalian spring. Niki sang a Greek song to herself on the steep path lined with acanthus. One needed to be
a gazelle to follow her, dashing around on her sturdy legs.
I glanced at Carol, white-haired and (lover of good food)
fat. She breathed hard, red in the face, toiling after Niki
without complaint. But then, who did complain? White
daisies grew in the grass, star flowers and marguerites,
spring in February. And the Tholos, glory of glories, its

purpose unknown, was a white circle of three columns where once had been twenty. *"Tout en marbre,"* said the French husband tenderly to his wife.

Up at the Stadium I was too numbed by the sudden cold to run another foot race. The enclosure, gigantic against the mountain, had seats for seven thousand. The shouting multitudes of pilgrims had pitched their tents nearby to attend the games. Here the prize was a crown not of olive but of laurel in honor of Apollo. "It was the festival of the goat," said Niki, her teeth chattering, and I burst into laughter at the white steam issuing in gusts from her mouth as she spoke in a frozen trance. She had turned into the Pythia.

To thaw out, we stopped at a café down the hill. It began to hail in a rapid tattoo on the window, changing to sleet and snow. Niki went on eating preserved cherries, explaining that Greeks offer them to a guest in the house. Soon, to please the women, we left the warm café to shop in the village where, quailing at the weather, I tried to fasten my apprehensive thoughts on the displays of "Greek art," uniformly ugly. At "The Delphic Corner," the owner George Petrou showed us a handwoven gray woolen suit, the replica of one he had sold ex-Queen Frederika. I refrained from buying such royal raiment as overweening. I already had an umbrella like the Queen of England's.

At 2:15 P.M. we filed uneasily into the bus to take leave of Delphi. Lunch had been late at the hotel, since Niki highhandedly changed the menu, ordering lamb cooked in the Greek style. How else was Carol the gourmet to write her cookbook?

The storm had become fearful. Parnassus had disappeared in cloud and so had we. Miles below, the Corinthian

Gulf shone silver in the sun. Creeping snail-like down the mountainside, we started the long journey to Athens. Snow piled up along the road. The place was lost now, no longer sacred, no longer *there*. Parnassus had withdrawn, grown hostile; winter had taken over and the sun god was gone. What folly to have come in February! Good-bye to Castalia, who wept as we passed great white frozen tears.

It grew worse, turning into a blizzard. Niki in the front seat stared motionless ahead, her knuckles white as she gripped her microphone. She showed no desire to distract Lambros as he crouched with tense muscles over the wheel. Surely they had been in this plight before? How slippery was the white vertical road? How *long* was the descent, from Phocis to Boeotia to Attica? Athens must be a hundred miles away ("164 miles, to be exact," B. said), and night would come. Well, the Four-Day Classical Tour had to be taken at your own risk. They never promised to bring you back alive.

A flock of black goats ahead refused to budge from the middle of the road. Snow fell over them like white fleece. I went on writing in my notebook for distraction: "A blizzard is not a thing of classical interest in Greece." "Somewhere I've read about the wolves of Parnassus, how they howl in the winter night."

Helen from Texas sat with eyes tight shut. Gordon stretched out as if asleep. The Herr leaned forward and, remarkably, spoke across the aisle to B. He expected soon to visit the state of Tennessee, he said. I prayed it was true, he would survive to pay a long happy visit to Tennessee. My God, my God, how it snowed!

We were coming to a snowbound hill village. "Arakova," Niki said, without turning her eyes from the road, "where rugs are made." Red, blue, green rugs, vivid in the snow-

storm, hung outside each shop in the narrow street. Stop
the bus! Stop, let us buy a rug. Let us buy *all* their rugs,
till the blizzard is over, till spring returns.

But Lambros drove straight through, reaching down to
switch on the radio for some bouzouki music. The people
of Arakova would hear it and think us revelers headed for
a night's carnival. Beyond the town a small local bus
loomed in front, stalled in the road. Lambros maneuvered
with difficulty around it, slipping, sliding, losing traction.
As he applied the brake we skidded sideways, nearly
ramming the guardrail. I saw him tremble with the effort
to control the plunging bus.

We inched down the mountain, with no choice but to go
wherever it led. For another ten, twenty, forty minutes, an
eternity, we went down, *down,* rocking, swerving, sweating
at the ordeal, emerging at last into—*what?* What was this?
Into a bright clear plateau. Into sudden sunshine.

The French wife screamed and hugged her mate. A gasp
ran through the bus. No snow had fallen here, though above
us the storm raged on. Lambros glanced at Niki and
clasped her hand. Both were obviously relieved, but Niki
sagged, seeming very tired. It was a dog's life being a
woman guide. I was one woman who didn't envy her.

"You remember Oedipus?" Niki called out. "Look
down, the bridge far below like a child's toy? There, at
the meeting of three roads, Oedipus killed his father on the
way from Delphi."

A gypsy family, strung out on donkeys, moved too slowly
from our path. Lambros blared his horn in frantic im-
patience. He would stop for nothing now we were beneath
the snow.

Ahead rose up Helicon with a rainbow round its shoulder. O, Niki! Not *another* mountain? Had we escaped

Parnassus only to leap to a new pinnacle? No doubt of it—
we began to climb round hairpin curves in a pink enchanted world of thousands of almond trees. This was
Helicon, abode of the Muses, with its wild thyme, beehives,
anemones, Helicon under a rainbow and it was spring.

Niki wanted us to see a Byzantine monastery. This one
was located below the summit, the monastery of St. Luke,
not the New Testament Luke but a local hermit and holy
man of the tenth century. In the courtyard, black-bearded
monks wandered about, fourteen resident here, unper-
turbed by the presence of a few women tourists.

The empty church with marble floors and walls of gold
mosaics was less splendid, Niki thought, than Daphni. I
liked the enormous black staring eyes of the Christ, the
round mournful eyes of his apostles. A small adjoining
room was being used as a church, for the monks were very
poor. When Niki entered this room, she crossed herself
three times, lighted a candle, carried it to the altar, crossed
herself three times more, and sighed deep in prayer. By
this time our group had filed inside. Niki shook herself,
collected her wits, and delivered a lecture on marriage.
"There is no civil marriage in Greece. Greeks may marry
within the church up to three times, following a death or
divorce. A priest may marry before becoming a priest only
if he has no plan to become a patriarch, who must be cervical
—cellular—what do I mean?" "Celibate," said B. "Celibate," said Niki, "from the start."

As she talked, an old white-bearded monk moved from
candle to candle with a long taper. He ignored us till Niki
paused, at which he stepped with effort onto a low platform, lifted his hand, and addressed us in English. "Marriage is necessary for health," he began. "Even among men
who will be priests it must be tolerated. We are human

flesh, alike in our desires. We need to love, forgive, understand each other. If we can talk by *numbers* [counting off one, two, three on his fingers], we can devise a common alphabet and common tongue. We can speak the same language of love under God."

Niki thanked him humbly in Greek. It was 4:30, and from outside the church a bell rang for prayer.

The women hurried to a "Greek art" shop across the courtyard, undismayed to find one doing business in a monastery. They went in search of goat bells. Niki put her hand on my arm and asked me to walk with her. As we passed again the Church of St. Luke, she pointed to still-broken windows from the German bombings when Hitler took over Greece and a swastika flew from the Acropolis. What she had to tell concerned that war. After leaving the monastery, we would drive through a nearby village where a monument had been erected in the square.

"I will show it only to you," said Niki. "You must say nothing, promise me. You must make no sign to the others."

Engraved there I would see the names of the 276 men and boys who had lived in the village, shot by the Germans in 1943 in reprisal for Greek resistance. Because of our three German companions, Niki kept silent. In her tact and compassion she withheld the tragic story.

At five that afternoon we started for Athens in a misty rain. I whispered Niki's tale to B., and we sat waiting to pass through the stricken town of Distomo. Niki waited too. Before she nodded, we had caught sight of the stark white pillar with its double column of names for the wives and children to read. Spring flowers gave a bold splash of color to the base. Niki looked back at us, her eyes wet, her face strained, and turned away. How many times in all these years had she wept to remember?

It grew dark as we raced down the mountain. I showed

Niki a magazine article I had brought along, Christopher Rand's "Guided Tour." On a visit to Greece Mr. Rand had taken this same tour, traveling in reverse order from Delphi to Corinth, in July not February. He had run into swarms of tourists, into blistering heat instead of blizzards. I wanted Niki to know his high praise of Greek women guides, a combination of mother, sister, teacher, nurse, diplomat, group leader, and geisha girl. Niki read in the poor light, laughing aloud.

"Geisha girl?" I whispered. She laughed again.

"Yes, yes, geisha girl. Why not? Everything."

Levadia, chief town of Boeotia, being noted for its shishkebab, we stopped for shishkebab—hot bites of lamb skewered on a wooden stick, the price of a hot dog at home. Dinner in Athens was at least two hours away. The Four-Day Classical Tour would be over.

Boarding the bus for the last time, I realized with a pang these were friends I must soon lose forever. Gordon and Judy would fly tomorrow to Naples. The French lovers were returning to Paris. Carol would continue around the world in eighty dishes. Her friend Zohmah was either going to or coming from Fiji. The Herr would travel for reasons of his own to Tennessee. B. and I were sailing on Monday across the Aegean to Istanbul, sailing to Byzantium. And Niki? She would sleep tomorrow to rest up for Monday's tour. Niki guided anywhere in Greece and the islands. In the summer season, March to November, she would be on tour in crowded buses, among multitudes at the ruins. This had been her life for the past seven years. Heroic Niki.

Well. In the dark the Frenchman kissed his wife an explosive smack. I turned in my seat and kissed B., trying to be quiet about it. "Bless you," he said. "Any time."

We were passing through Thebes. I peered out dutifully at a lighted taverna. Nothing remained of the ancient city,

Niki said, though were it there we couldn't have seen it.
What did I know of Thebes? Seven were against it; Alexander destroyed it (for which the Greeks never forgave
him), leveling the city to smoking ruins "when temple and
tower went to the ground"—save for one house he left
standing, Pindar's. I liked that story. Pausanias saw the
remains of his house only seventeen centuries ago. 44 miles
to Athens.

We entered Attica about 8:00. The bus had become
hushed, Niki silent for a long time. In our headlights two
foxes rushed across the road. We passed a lighted roadside
shrine for travelers. Thanks for survival.

"Hello," said Niki into her microphone. "Over your
heads, on top the mountain, Dionysus was born."

Total silence in the bus.

"Oh, my children. Don't tell me you've forgot Dionysus,
god of wine?"

Not a sound. Apparently we were asleep. I nodded my
head, yes, I remember, and closed my eyes.

I thought to myself: incredible Niki. She has bound us
together, achieved the miracle. For four days no one was
mean or spoiled the party. No disasters occurred, no dis-
appointments. We too have shown stamina, endurance,
patience, following her example. We are a valiant, courteous company, we have worn well—schoolteachers, doctor,
gourmet, lovers alike. We can boast an electronics engineer
(Gordon) and a descendant of Anne Bradstreet. Together
we sought Greece's glory and found it—five assorted men,
eleven women, four languages. I personally had found
more besides: call it peace. I regretted the journey's end.

We had made up an envelope for Niki, and Carol chose
this moment near Athens to give it to her. I wouldn't like
being tipped, perhaps no more did Niki. The word "guide"
was inadequate and wrong. She had more dignity, far more

knowledge than the word implied. But we meant well, and all fourteen passengers had contributed.

"Thank you, my children," said Niki. There was an envelope for Lambros. "He thanks you and wishes he could speak your language." Lambros added something in Greek that made Niki laugh. "He says to tell you if I am your mother he is very happy to be your father."

Streetlights began to appear, the road broadened to a highway. A large electric sign near the harbor shifted from red to green, from Greek to English. When green it said "Metaxa Brandy." We were on the Sacred Way, passing the church at Daphni where we started four days ago. The circle was complete.

Athens looked well illuminated tonight, with Mt. Lycabettus and the floodlit Parthenon blazing against the sky. I recalled a story from Athenaeus about a visit of Mark Antony to Athens, when from the Acropolis he saw the entire city lighted in his honor with torches hung from every roof.

One thing I still needed to know. After a little prodding, B. leaned over and spoke to the Herr across the aisle.

"Would you mind, sir, telling me what your occupation is?"

"I beg your pardon."

"Your work? Your employment at home?" In kindness B. didn't add, "My wife is nosy. She put me up to this."

"Professor," he answered shortly.

"Of what, may I ask?"

"Chemistry."

"Thank you."

Constitution Square, with crowds and café tables, looked festive on Saturday night. We drew up first to the luxurious Grande Bretagne to let out Gordon and Judy. Judy kissed me good-bye. The chances were we might never meet, but we would exchange Christmas cards. The King George came next, and the German couple prepared to depart. The wife, stolid to the last, lumbered down the aisle in her tall beaver hat and climbed heavily from the bus without a smile, a glance, a word for anyone. Niki stopped her husband at the door.

"I am sorry I was unable to speak your language. I hope you enjoyed the tour."

"I did." His tone was curt. "I brought along a guidebook to Greece and I studied it." No thanks to Niki. No nod. No good-bye.

Rosemarie left alone. "I'll be back, dear Niki," she said with an embrace. "It was vunderful and so are you. Look out for me next year, same time, same tour."

Finally the French couple and we were left, the last passengers on the bus. Niki kissed us in the French style on both cheeks. She touched our faces as if memorizing them.

"*Au revoir, mes enfants,*" she said. "Good-bye, my dear friends."

I held in my hand the withered asphodel. Niki reached down to her seat and gave me her two branches of flowering almond from Mt. Helicon. I seemed to part from a life-long friend, whom I loved, who had given her love freely to me and to the rest, the only family she had. It hurt to let her go.

I stepped down from the bus and walked with B. into the Hotel Alexiou, knowing that unless I made a habit of visiting Greece for its classical tours I would never see her again. Miss Niki Camara, Plutarch Street, Athens—I would never see her again.

This piece, Niki, is for you.

The Belly Button

"There is no Omphalos, either in the center of the
earth or of the sea. If any there be, it is visible to the
gods, not visible to mortals."
—EPIMENIDES OF CRETE

Epimenides of Crete was reckoned wise,
A sage, a sophist, so oracular
That to him certain truths have been attributed,
Such as the saying, "Cretans are always liars."

A bold unraveler of lie from legend,
He argued furthermore, "There is no Omphalos,"
No navel of this earth, no belly button—
At least none visible to him, a mortal.

A human world, without umbilicus?
So reasoned Epimenides, who had never
Like Buddha contemplated his own navel,
Or else denied he had one, being Cretan.

Byzantium Without Yeats

Yeats never went to Byzantium—or to Constantinople, Istanbul, Stamboul, whatever you want to call it. Though he said he did,

> And therefore I have sailed the seas and come
> To the holy city of Byzantium

he never crossed those seas (the Mediterranean, Ionian, Aegean, Sea of Marmara) to reach the Bosphorus and the Golden Horn where mosques and graceful minarets against the skyline of the old city of Byzantium glow in the distance, the dome of St. Sophia glitters yellow gold in the sunlight.

He evoked a Byzantium that never was. Byzantium was the heaven of his mind, the holy city of his imagination, even though he said he envisioned the actual city in the time of Justinian, sixth century A.D., when the greatest of Byzantine emperors became sole ruler of the eastern Roman Empire. Yeats imagined himself an inhabitant walking its streets. He called it a place of purification where he would forget the flesh and bodily desire. (Did he know it was ravaged by bubonic plague in Justinian's time, with half the Byzantines dead?)

Justinian was a Macedonian peasant who ruled supreme and absolute in power, the elect of God. His barbaric empress Theodora, daughter of a bear-keeper, was a former actress and prostitute, who ruled with him in equal majesty, "as though the Roman Empire lay at her feet." Procopius in his *Secret History* told the story in considerable detail (and, I hope, in hyperbole) of Theodora's scandalous life

as mistress of sexual vice, calling her bestial, cruel, licen-
tious, base, dissolute, infamous, the most shameful of
women. As an actress, one of her lewd roles was a burlesque
performance of Leda and the swan. As a wanton with count-
less lovers, said Procopius, she would attend a party with
ten or more muscular young men, lie with them the night
long, and having reduced them to exhaustion turn to their
servants, thirty on occasion. In total depravity she plied
her trade with her whole body: "And though she made use
of three openings, she used to take Nature to task, complaining that it had not pierced her breasts with larger
holes so that it might be possible for her to contrive another
method of copulation there." While she was not yet twenty,
people passing her on the street drew aside from contact
with a creature so impure. Gibbon, in the *Decline and Fall*,
added discreet footnotes in Greek to reveal her insatiable
lusts.

(Fortunately, Yeats never chose Theodora as a poetic
symbol of Maud Gonne, though both were strikingly beautiful, both imperious. Theodora had bold black eyes, a pale
face, a small graceful body. Maud Gonne was called the
most beautiful woman in Ireland.)

A lavish spender, Justinian rebuilt Constantinople into
magnificence. But he didn't encourage learning, and he did
abolish the Academy of Plato. By Justinian's time, the imperial library founded by Constantine had gone up in
smoke, including a copy of Homer written in gold on a
snakeskin 120 feet long. There were no poets in his reign.
Poetry and learning were idle pursuits that did nothing to
replenish his treasury for the costly wars waged against
the Persians, the Vandals in Africa, the Goths in Italy.

Justinian reigned as despoiler and tyrant. Under him
slavery existed and such wretched poverty that in January,

532, there arose an angry mob who, in one fearful day of rioting, burned much of the city, including St. Sophia, Church of Holy Wisdom built by Constantine; including the gateway of the Great Palace. In reprisal some thirty thousand people were put to death in the Hippodrome by the King's soldiers.

War, pestilence, famine marked his rule, which was disgraced, wrote Gibbon, "by a visible decrease of the human species." Procopius said of his reign, "There was no laughter in life." And at his death his empire ended with him.

Yet Justinian's masterpiece, in a golden age of architecture, was the new St. Sophia with its grandeur of polished marbles and gold mosaics, built to replace the older temple now a heap of ruins. "It is my custom," said Justinian, "to do whatever is pious and righteous." He planned St. Sophia to be the fairest church in the world, erected by "the equal of the Apostles," dedicated to Christ in His Wisdom and the glory of Mary, Mother of God. "Solomon, I have outdone you!" cried Justinian at its completion in 537, stunned by the genius of it.

Yeats never saw "the gold mosaic of a wall" or the "marbles of the dancing floor" he made his Byzantium poems about, conspicuous though they are today in a Moslem world. He never saw the miracle of St. Sophia, temple of holy wisdom (where he might well inquire, as anyone might, "*Whose* holiness? *Which* wisdom?"). It had been a temple of Diana before Constantine built it and Justinian, nearly fifteen hundred years ago, rebuilt it into this splendor of veined marbles, jasper, pillars of porphyry. From Byzantine to Christian to Moslem, from church to mosque to museum—Which gods? Whose wisdom?

Now St. Sophia is Islamic, the cross supplanted by the crescent. Immense yellow discs on the walls contain holy words in black sworls from the Koran. When the Turks captured Byzantium in 1453, they stabled their camels in the temple and kept their prostitutes there, barn and brothel. They danced in priests' robes, hid the Byzantine icons under whitewash and plaster, added a minaret to each of the four angles of the cathedral and turned the face of holy wisdom toward Mecca.

As I stood in St. Sophia under the suffused yellow light of the gold dome—from which no Christ Pantocrater, no radiant Cross, no fluttering pigeons (that Justinian called the messengers of God) shone down on us; from which no longer sounded Yeats's "great cathedral gong"—a clamorous argument broke out between an American tourist and a Turkish guide. The American had made a tactless remark, stating in clear tones his conviction that throughout history conquerors have been guilty of desecrating temples.

"In the name of God the greatest crimes have been committed," he observed briskly. The Turkish guide took violent exception to his words.

"Moslems do not desecrate!" he shouted, shaking his fist in the man's face. "Others, yes. But not we, not Moslems!"

Both men glared in speechless anger. It was a squabble fit for a marketplace. Yet I saw what the American meant. The Turks had turned even the Parthenon into a mosque (in 1456) and two centuries later used it as a powder magazine during a bombardment by the Venetians, till a shell from that battle blew out the temple and threw down its columns. In St. Sophia one was bound to reflect on the history of conquest. In this holy city of the imagination.

Settled by Greek colonists, first it had been Greek Byzantium. By Constantine's time, already nearly a thousand years old, it became for eleven more centuries Constantinople, capital of the Christian Roman world, astride two continents. In the fifteenth century the Turks took over, and in the twentieth the hotelkeepers.

Yeats might think twice before sailing (in person) to Byzantium. Where are its artificers now? Would he find them in the Covered Bazaar, that huge labyrinth of ninety-two streets completely roofed over, overflowing with goldsmiths, silversmiths, coppersmiths, jewelers, embroiderers, slipper sellers, rug merchants, silk merchants, leather merchants, dealers in glittering brass and antique swords? All those goldsmiths and artificers—"The golden smithies of the Emperor!" All those wheedlers and cheats.

There is today the lovely Blue Mosque of Sultan Ahmed, but it was never Byzantine, no saints hovering, no "sages standing in God's holy fire"—a purely Moslem heaven, a blue paradise of Mohammed. Still, the pigeons do fly about like the Holy Ghost under that celestial blue dome. Would Yeats be tempted to set these Turkish pigeons on a new golden bough in Istanbul?

"I have read somewhere" (Yeats made note) "that in the Emperor's palace at Byzantium was a tree made of gold and silver, and artificial birds that sing."

Of the Great Palace built by Constantine, enlarged by Justinian, little remains: a few fragments of masonry, a mosaic pavement. There the Emperor, dressed in stiff brocade with a gilded beard, sat on the throne of Solomon. But it was a later emperor than Justinian—Theophilus of Byzantium (829–842)—who enhanced the Great Palace by adding a golden plane tree, its boughs heavy with artificial birds waving their golden wings, while under the tree stood two massive gold lions. By a mechanical device, the birds sang and the lions roared.

This was the actual tree Yeats had in mind, on whose branches he himself meant to perch, a poet of Byzantium, as a golden metal singing bird

> Of hammered gold and gold enamelling
> To keep a drowsy Emperor awake;
> Or set upon a golden bough to sing
> To lords and ladies of Byzantium
> Of what is past, or passing, or to come.

Instead of the Great Palace, on view now is the Topkopi Palace or Grand Seraglio of the sultans, with emeralds and rubies the size of hen's eggs. Byron, who did in fact sail to Byzantium in 1810 and stayed two months, visited the Sultan's Palace, but he was revolted by the sight beneath its gloomy walls of two dogs gnawing a dead body. Disliking the Turks, sickened and appalled by filth and cruelty, bored with the mosques and bazaars, Byron was unmoved to poetry. His city was Venice not Constantinople, "the greenest city of my imagination."

I can't recommend the Pera Palace either (where I stayed in Istanbul). In better days among the swank hostelries of the world, it resembles an emperor's palace where a people's bloody revolution has occurred after which the people moved in. It is elegant but scarred. The floors are marble, the public rooms filled with florid *objets d'art*, Persian vases, Turkish divans, taborets of mother-of-pearl, crystal chandeliers. In March, 1941, during World War II, a bomb exploded in the lobby and burned out the first floor. The Pera Palace faces Byzantium across the shimmer of the Bosphorus, toward the old city built on hills, a sweep of housetops, domes, and minarets like rocket missiles against the sky. In Justinian's day, instead of minarets, tall monumental columns were topped by statues of the emperors. ("Monuments of unageing intellect.")

Nor would Yeats discover the sages of Byzantium, the singing-masters of his soul, at the fabulous Istanbul-Hilton, lavish but out of tune with its sea-green carpet stretching over the luxurious lounge like a Roman stage-set by Fellini; with its orchestra playing "Night and Day" and a sleek young Turk trying to sound like Frank Sinatra. ("Soul clap its hands and sing.")

Yeats would have to adjust his imagination to this holy city of Byzantium like the rest of us. Recently I read in a guidebook to Turkey a sensible piece of advice, useful in the end to tourists and poets both: "To feel at home in Istanbul, one must exert a certain accommodation power."

Or there was a road sign I saw once in Macedonia that said, "Respect the limitations."

A Tourist to Byzantium

And so, Yeats, I have sailed the seas and come
To the holy city of Byzantium,
Not by your dark seas, mistier than mine.
I crossed the Atlantic on the Italian line
Aboard the old *Vulcania,* while you went
Upon a dolphin's back more confident
Astraddle him of paradise than some,
Like me, a tourist to Byzantium.
I sailed in ships the real, well-charted seas
With maps to indicate the Cyclades,
Cruising for days the Mediterranean Sea,
The Ionian Sea, and the Aegean Sea,
Seeking the heaven of the mind I want
Myself, as you did; crossing the Hellespont,
The Sea of Marmara, the Bosphorus,
By straits and routes you never traveled, thus
To reach at last the Golden Horn and come
By so much water to Byzantium—
Only to meet no golden codgers now,
No singing-masters of my soul, no bough
Of gold enameled birds on hand to sing
That summoned you to paradise. Nothing!
Nothing but Turks in Istanbul. *Nothing.*

Where Did All the Blue Go, Picasso?

By the age of ninety, Picasso had become a monument of his own making. In this Age of Picasso, he was no longer a man but a work created by his hands in his own image. A few years before his death, he presented a sculpture to the city of Chicago, where he had never been. *"C'est un don, un cadeau pour Chicago,"* he said, a fifty-foot monument for the plaza of the Civic Center. Nobody knew what it was, and still nobody knows. It had no name. Could it be an effigy of the artist, Picasso himself? Some said no, it was an eagle in flight. Or a vulture at rest. Maybe a blindfolded goddess weighing scales. Maybe a *nothing?* Some said, "No, don't ask what it is. It's Picasso" (echoing his friend Cocteau: "When you see a woman who hasn't an eye where she ought to have one, you don't say: 'there's a woman who hasn't an eye where she ought to have one.' You say 'Picasso!' ").

A bystander wondered, "Is Picasso pulling our leg?" He was told, "Oh, I don't think so. I think he must be serious."

Apparently no one said, "It's ugly." It is ugly. It looks like a winged donkey with close-set eyes. A moose. A baboon. An Indian in a queer war bonnet. Picasso was asked if by chance he had Chicago in mind when he made the design. *"Peut-être,"* he said.

To call it ugly is not to condemn it. In our time Beauty and the Beast have become identical. If the hideous and grotesque, the evil and lunatic, look beautiful to us, Picasso may be in fact responsible:

Lastly, Picasso has blasted to rubble the aesthetic differentiation between the Beautiful and the Ugly and has, tempo-

119

rarily, at any rate, disposed of the notion that true art is an imitation of nature.

—*Times Literary Supplement*, December 22, 1961

What is Beauty now? Cocteau explained: "When Picasso hurls magnificent insults at the human face, they're not really insults." Fair is foul and foul is fair. The human face benefits from having its features dislocated, its harmony destroyed.

Wallace Stevens, in "The Man with the Blue Guitar," asked what Picasso has done to us:

> Is this picture of Picasso's, this "hoard
> Of destructions," a picture of ourselves,
>
> Now, an image of our society?
> Do I sit, deformed, a naked egg . . . ?

An image of our society? Certainly it is. Aren't we indeed a "hoard of destructions"? Stevens was only using Picasso's own words: "A picture used to be a sum of additions. With me a picture is a sum of destructions." His attack on humanity was ruthless, demonic, and, to him, reasonable. *La belle laide.*

Once in our innocence we sought the Beautiful and the Sublime. Think of Gainsborough and Reynolds, who painted every woman beautiful. It took Picasso to change the course of modern art. "I will tell you one of Picasso's greatest secrets," wrote Cocteau. "He runs faster than beauty. That is why his creatures look ugly."

And E. E. Cummings agreed, though reluctantly,

> Picasso
> you give us Things
> which
> bulge . . .

> bodies lopped
> of every
> prettiness

Yet the early pictures, those of Picasso's blue period, were touchingly beautiful. They had the beauty of compassion and pity for the thin pierrots and harlequins, the hungry beggars, the blind men, for the sad *maternités, les pauvres, les misérables*. They grieved for the solitary outcasts of this world. There was love in them.

Picasso used a lot of blue in those days, suffusing his pictures with blue, because it's said he was too poor to buy other colors. When he made money and took a mistress to support, then another and another—Fernande, Eva, Olga, who became his first wife, Marie-Thérèse, Dora, Françoise, Jacqueline—his outlook changed. The blue changed with it, moving toward rose, deepening into red: into brutal distortions of the human form, phantoms, scrambled images, into freaks and two-faced women, fury and violence and ugliness. ("What can I add to that?" asked Picasso. "I've said it all.")

After *Les Demoiselles d'Avignon* of 1907, a picture of five naked women so bizarre it shocked even his artist friends, Picasso prospered. Flinging breasts about and buttocks, disassembling and rearranging the eyes, the nose, the private parts, he gave the world a look at itself, and we agreed it is an excellent likeness. Yet the only lady I have ever seen whose beauty was flawless with two cracked ears and one eye missing was Queen Nefertiti.

John Donne would have denied that the beautiful and the ugly are alike. Quite the opposite. He assumed he knew the meaning of beauty. When his mistresses were fair of face, they were always kind. When they were ugly, they were harsh and cruel. Christ, therefore, since he was beautiful like the fair mistresses would be compassionate and kind to Donne:

> so I say to thee:
> To wicked spirits are horrid shapes assigned;
> This beauteous form assures a piteous mind.

Shakespeare understood the simple difference between the two merely by looking at Silvia:

> Who is Silvia? What is she,
>   That all our swains commend her?
> Holy, fair, and wise is she;
>   The heaven such grace did lend her,
> That she might admired be.
>
> Is she kind as she is fair?
>   For beauty lives with kindness.

When I Haven't Any Blue, I Use Red

(*A remark made by Picasso*)

Shall we say Woe for having absolutely no
Blue in the house?
No ultramarine, cobalt, turquoise, sapphire, azure, or indigo
Blue at the easel
For this bloody old world
Daubed red as a measle?
No cerulean dye
For love's rubyred eye?
Where did all the blue go,
Picasso?

Byron on a Diet

In 1806 Byron weighed 202 pounds (he was five feet eight). By wearing seven waistcoats and a greatcoat to play cricket till he sweated to exhaustion, by taking hot baths, eating one meal a day, swallowing physic, "my clothes," he said, "have been taken in nearly a yard."

He was eighteen years old, enrolled at Trinity College, Cambridge. Being too fat made him gloomy, dieting depressed his spirits. "I consider myself as destined never to be happy," he wrote a school friend. "I am an isolated Being in the earth, without a Tie to attach me to life, except a few School-fellows. and a score of females."

> Weary of love. of life, devoured with spleen,
> I rest, a perfect Timon not nineteen.

Only a score of females, underlined. Poor chap. By the next year when *Hours of Idleness* was published, a slim volume of poems by a slim young man, Byron had become Byronic, stormy with passion and self-confidence:

> Oh! might I kiss those eyes of fire,
> A million scarce would quench desire:
> Still would I steep my lips in bliss,
> And dwell an age in every kiss . . .
> To part would be a vain endeavour:
> Could I desist? ah! never—never!

For the next ten years the transformation was heroic, and as it proved historic. By dieting he affected the whole Romantic Movement. A fat Byron—ah! never—never! It would be a more dampening sight than a too solid Apollo

Belvidere. Love kept his weight down or (to quote *Don Juan*) that "No less imperious passion, Self-love." Ever after, for the rest of his life, he waged a mighty but intermittent struggle to stay thin, alternating from skeleton to fat man and back again. At intervals despairing of his figure, he starved himself, fasting to excess: a cup of tea for breakfast, a cup of tea for supper, a light vegetable dinner doused in vinegar, plus a dose of Epsom salts. He chewed tobacco to forget his hunger. And his face, said Scott, was pale "like an alabaster vase." Thus the reports of Byron's friends as to his size, shape, and appearance differ sharply from year to year, one from the other:

John Galt remembered him in the moonlight in 1810 in a boat carrying him to Malta, looking lean and "apparitional," "a mystery in a winding sheet, crowned with a halo."

1817. A gorgeous slender Byron in Rome so alarmed Lady Liddell, a friend of Lady Byron's, that she told her daughter, "Don't look at him. He is dangerous to look at!"

1818. In this year Byron at tl. ty was grown puffy and stout, jaded, dejected, no longer quite so ravishing:

> By now at thirty years my hair is grey.
> (I wonder what it will be like at forty?
> I thought of a peruke the other day).

By adding eating to his other vices, "He had grown very fat," wrote Newton Hanson from Venice, "his shoulders broad and round, and the knuckles of his hands were lost in fat." The Montgomerys, also in Venice, reported him "Extremely fat, bloated and heavy." From England, Augusta Leigh noted in distress, "I hear he looks very well, but *fat*, immensely large, and his hair long."

1819. Thomas Moore was startled to observe Byron's

corpulence. "He had grown fatter both in person and face. . . . He was still, however, eminently handsome."

1821. His friend Trelawny noticed a decided shrinkage: "His terror of getting fat was so great that he reduced his diet to the point of absolute starvation . . . he resolved to keep down to eleven stone [154 pounds] or shoot himself." No doubt Byron was haunted by the memory of his mother, so obese that she rolled in her gait. His diet consisted of biscuits and soda water. Each morning he measured the size of his wrists and waist. He was bad-tempered and hungry.

1822 (June). Leigh Hunt: "Upon seeing Lord Byron, I hardly knew him, he was grown so fat."

1822 (September). Thomas Medwin: ". . . he has starved himself into an unnatural thinness." To keep up his stamina, Byron now drank a pint of gin every night instead of the earlier vinegar and water. "Why don't you drink, Medwin?" he said. "Gin-and-water is the source of all my inspiration."

Yet in this year he was still remarkably beautiful, still Byronic. Trelawny saw him in Florence, "without a stain or furrow on his pallid skin, his shoulders broad, chest open, body and limbs finely proportioned." He wore a blue tartan braided jacket, a blue velvet cap with a gold band on his curly hair, loose nankeen trousers strapped down to cover his feet. He had, said Trelawny, the form and features of a god.

1823. Lady Blessington's intense desire to meet Byron was satisfied when she visited Italy the year Byron was thirty-five. She expressed keen disappointment at his ordinary appearance, which fell far short of her expectations, though she had written in her diary the day before they met, "I hope he may not be fat, as Moore described him at

Venice: for a *fat poet* is an anomaly in my opinion." On April 1, 1823, together with her husband and her dashing companion Count d'Orsay, she paid a call on the poet at the Casa Saluzzo in Genoa where he had been living for the last few months. "I have seen Lord Byron; and am disappointed." She found him puny, exceedingly thin, down to a "skeleton thinness." His hair was streaked with gray. His clothes hung loose on a skinny frame. He weighed 149 pounds.

Only twelve months later, April 19, 1824, Byron died at Missolonghi. He died a handsome, slender Romantic, tragic in death—not from starvation, not from pride, not for love, but "that Greece might still be free."

The Seasonable Mr. White of Selborne

The way to be happy in London in the spring is to spend one's days in the British Museum, reading the manuscript of the Journals of Gilbert White. Except for a small selection, they have never been printed—ten thousand daily records, twenty-five years (1768–1793) of the serenest life I've ever envied. Mr. White of Selborne is my peace.

It was cold in London in May. The traffic signs "Walk warily" were getting on my nerves. They reminded me I was an alien registered with the police. *Walk warily.* My God, I try to. The lovers in Bloomsbury Square wore leather jackets, tight pants, long hair, boy and girl alike. A sign in a London bus said: "If you are in despair or tempted to suicide and do not know where to turn for help, ring—" Automatically I memorized the number. What would Mr. White of Selborne think of a world as desperate as mine?

A man of his composure belonged in Selborne, the tiny Hampshire village where he lived and died, first taking care to be born on the premises. There, with world enough and time, in a town of no Papists and no dissenters, he was content to want no more. When he visited London perhaps once a year, he caught cold and developed a rash. For even a brief stay, he would arrange to have sent up twelve braces of cucumber from his Selborne garden. He kept an extremely meager journal in London with little to report and little birdsong, nothing but the promiscuous pigeons so crowded together in temptation they were "apt to forget the rules of strict chastity, and follow too often the example of people in high life."

I went one day to the British Museum expecting to spend an hour glancing through the diaries. Instead I stayed a month, going each morning to sit before a book rack in the Manuscript Room, forbidden to leave the journal for a moment unattended or lay my hands across its fragile pages. Having acquired the manuscript a century after Mr. White's death, the Museum labeled it "select." That meant precious.

It was a printed calendar called a "Naturalist's Journal," one week to a page, each page ruled into narrow columns for daily entry of wind and weather, with a wide column at the right for "Miscellaneous Observations and Memorandums." Here Mr. White soon got to the heart of the matter. As a miscellaneous observer he found his calling. Beginning in 1781, he inserted a blank sheet between each page of the Journal for the growing number of his observations and memorandums. He had mastered the art: he saw and recorded.

It became the natural history of his life. A rejoicer, a thriving, easyminded man, he lived during the reigns of the three Georges in a changing world as violent as my own. Such events as the American Revolution, the French Revolution, and the industrial revolution heaved the planet. Yet while men struggled, Mr. White turned his mind to the harvest mouse and wrote with his usual civility the life history of the field cricket. To the trumpet-like honk of the goose he assigned no blame; this was the only honk the goose had. He was never in a hurry. His diary contained no complaint, no blots, no sense of ill winds, but a lot about earthworms.

On the intelligence of earthworms, Darwin later wrote: "There is little to say on this head." Gilbert White with customary grace rose to their defense: "Earthworms, though in appearance a small and despicable link in the chain of nature, yet, if lost, would make a lamentable chasm."

July 1, 1775: When earthworms lie out a nights on the turf, though they extend their bodies a great way, they do not quite leave their holes but keep the ends of their tails fixed therein; so that on the least alarm they can retire with precipitation under the earth. . . . Even in copulation their hinder parts never quit their holes: so that no two except they lie within reach of each other's bodies can have any commerce of that kind; but as every individual is an hermaphrodite, there is no difficulty in meeting with a mate: as would be the case were they of different sexes.

That was the authentic sound of his voice—scrupulous to note, courteous and mild, simple but elegant. His world resembled Eden, never trivial, extraordinarily calm. He measured its rainfall and loved its dew, abided its house-flies. He knew its trees and the ground he walked on. Like James Thomson he wrote "The Seasons," and the virtue of each year of his life was that it was seasonable.

Like Thoreau he took pleasure simply in the nature of a day. But I think Mr. White would have called Thoreau's two-year sojourn at Walden a bit hasty, an overnight stay, a flying visit. Thoreau's journal, too, in fourteen volumes might have struck him as unmercifully longwinded, since his own was terse, limited most often to a word or two, with an entry like "Green gooseberries" or "Blue stinking mist."

In January, almost any January, Mr. White carried hot dung to his cucumber bed, tubbed and pickled a young fat hog. The nuthatch chattered. Snowdrops and hepatica began to blow, ivy berries swelled, turnip greens came in.

Jupiter shone or Venus was resplendent. Peter Wells's well ran over.

Jan. 18, 1784: Clouds put up their heads.

By February the missel thrush was pleased to sing, and Mr. White received three gallons of the best French brandy from London. Peter Wells's well ran over.

Feb. 28, 1769: Raven sits.

The woodpecker laughed in March. Beetles buzzed. Horse ants hurried forth and frogs spawned. He sent Mr. White of Newton some male cucumber blossoms in a box. Come April the singing of birds was everywhere: the stone curlew whistled, the willow wren made a plaintive note, the turtle cooed, the cuckoo cried, the wryneck piped, the grasshopper lark whispered, the nightingale sang in Honey Lane. In hyacinth weather Timothy the tortoise (a legacy left him by his aunt, Mrs. Snooke) emerged from under the laurel hedge and, in a spirit of inquiry, Mr. White took Timothy's pulse, which was imperceptible; nearly drowned him in a tub of water to see if he could swim; tootled on a trumpet in his ear (he didn't seem to regard the noise); and failed to discover his sex, which was female. Timothy never laid an egg.

Apr. 4, 1785: Butterfly.

Swifts arrived in May during the bottling out of the port wine, and his niece Clement was brought to bed of her fifth child, a boy. Though a bachelor himself, a little upright man with an expressive eye, Mr. White took as pleased a note of the rising number of his nephews and nieces as if they were so many titmice or water wagtails.

May 21, 1769: White owls have young.

The harmonies of June brought male glowworms attracted by candlelight to his parlor. The fern owl chattered, the wood owl hooted, swallows pursued and buffeted the magpies, golden-crown wrens brought forth their broods, the redstart sang on the maypole. Swifts stayed out till ten minutes to nine, dashing round church and tower in little parties, squeaking as they went.

June 14, 1776: I saw two swifts, entangled with each other, fall out of their nest to the ground, from whence they soon rose and flew away. This accident was probably owing to amorous dalliance. Hence it appears that swifts when down can rise again.

During July Mr. White gathered lavender. Swallows fed their young in the air. Female ants, big with egg, came out from under the stairs. Timothy the tortoise skulked "amidst the umbrageous forests of the asparagus beds."

When Sister Barker with nieces Mary and Elizabeth visited him in August, the harvest bugs bit the ladies. Bulls began to make their shrill autumnal note; in the full moon rams paid court to the ewes; bats were breeding under the tiles of his house. While the swans flounced and dived, he cut 424 cucumbers in one week in September. Timothy the tortoise retired to the laurel hedge to lay up for the winter. Five gallons and one pint of brandy arrived from London.

Sept. 20, 1782: One little starveling wasp.

By October the air was full of gossamer, here and there a straggling swallow. 46 ravens flew over the hanger. Golden larches lit up November, a bee was on the asters. After the servants had gone to bed, the kitchen hearth swarmed with crickets the size of fleas.

Nov. 24, 1788: Wheeled dung.

On Christmas Day a water wagtail frequented Wolmer Pond. Peter Wells's well started to run over. A fox ran up the street of Selborne at noonday.

Yet, as Mr. White ever knew, though seasons return they also pass. A favorite line of his was from Geffrey Whitney's "Emblemes" (1586): "And all must ende that ever was begonne." The year 1793 marked the time of the Terror in Paris. On Jan. 21, while Louis XVI was beheaded by the guillotine, the song thrush sang. Mr. White's nephews and nieces now living numbered 62. On Feb. 1, as the Republic of France declared war against England and Holland, he tubbed and salted a fine young hog. March brought the dog-toothed violets, April the sound of the cuckoo once more. In May two nightingales sang in the outlet. By June Mr. White barely had time to record the presence of the fiery lily, the cinnamon rose, peonies in bloom.

On June 14, his friend Mr. John Mulso came for a visit. Next day, in his graceful and unhurried penmanship, Mr. White wrote the final entry.

June 15, 1793: Men wash their sheep. Mr. J. Mulso left us.

He had numbered the days of the following week, June 16–22, preparing to live and write serenely on. It never came about. Mr. White died on June 26, at peace with himself and all the world. He asked to be buried outdoors.

There was, his neighbors said, no harm in this man.

(Louis XVI, beheaded that year, spent much of his time in the woods and fields and, like Mr. White of Selborne, kept a journal. Between 1775 and 1789 he ran down 1,274 stags. His journal entries, like Mr. White's, were terse, so brief that for most days the entry was "Nothing." On July 14, 1789, when the Bastille was stormed, he wrote for that day "Nothing."

It was a personal diary—to record when he took medicine or went to Mass, especially when he hunted stags. It noted his head colds, hemorrhoids, dinners and balls, expenses, the stunning proof of an empty life. On Bastille Day, he may have meant he didn't hunt that morning, or that he shot nothing. Even so, the entry stands: *"Rien."*)

"What make ye of Parson White in Selborne?" inquired Carlyle in 1832. Coleridge, for one, made sense of him. In the British Museum I found a copy of the 1802 edition of Gilbert White's *Works* (*The Natural History of Selborne* plus selections from the Journal), which looked like a cookbook, bound presumably by Mrs. Wordsworth in a piece of her blue-flowered cotton gown.

This Coleridge read and annotated, agreeing in genial footnotes with the "sweet delightful book." One memorandum, however, he read with incredulity, finding it not only inaccurate but ridiculous:

Dec. 13, 1789: One of my neighbours shot a ring-dove on an evening just as it was returning from feed and going to roost. When his wife had picked and drawn it, she found its craw stuffed with the most nice and tender tops of turnips. These she washed and boiled, and so sat down to a choice and delicate plate of greens, culled and provided in this extraordinary manner.

Nonsense! snorted Coleridge. On the margin he wrote heavily in ink: "A *plate* of greens found in the craw of a Ring-dove ! ! A *peck* of Turnip Tops would, when boiled, make little more."

Some people say that Gilbert White discovered the formula for happiness. A. Edward Newton, the book collector, was one who declared this to be true but added, "He died before making the announcement, leaving it for me to do so." With reckless courage, Mr. Newton then tried to state the formula (not one to be passed on idly), missing the point altogether, hitting wide of the mark. "It is to be very busy with the unimportant," said Mr. Newton.

Gilbert White was a busy man but it was with the miraculous. To read him is to find one's own world mended. I think it's the way he steadies the mind.

Mr. White, Walking

"My little intelligence is confined to the
  narrow sphere of my own observations at home."

Mr. White of Selborne, walking, walking,
Met the miraculous. It was there
Like the pink hepaticas in his garden,
Like the Hampshire swallows, everywhere.

Owls hooted at him in B flat, purely,
Nightingales sang, all at concert pitch.
Even the echoes were polysyllabic.
Mr. White measured an echo which

Shouted in Latin: *Monstrum horrendum,
Informe, ingens*—and said no more,
Meaning no insolence. Titmice loved him.
Squirrels left their hazelnuts by his door.

Daily he noted the flora and fauna
Of a world tuned like a mellow chime
To the miraculous, waking its echoes
Ten learned syllables at a time.

Mr. White of Selborne, walking, walking,
Had but to listen. Punctually, then,
The cuckoo struck a D sharp at evening.
Two fierce quick notes sang the willow wren.

(When Mr. White tested the echoes on nearby Noar Hill,
he spoke in Latin to make sure nobody was tricking him.)

Beautiful Lofty Gardeners

Gardeners are happy people. Whether they are born sanguine and by accident take up gardening, or whether this calling makes them merry and benign I don't know. Yet come spring and, like lovers, lunatics, and poets, here come the gardeners—these days the organic gardeners with their love of compost heaps and their lore of ladybugs. In cheerful garden books they write Virgil's *Georgics* over again: "Scorn not to soak the dry soil with fattening dung." "Pray for dripping midsummers and clear winters, O husbandmen." They sound busily at peace like Gilbert White of Selborne, whose common entry in his Journal was "Wheeled dung." Like Thoreau they plant their nine bean rows, scorning murder by insecticides, undismayed by the wanton ways of the world, maintaining a state of grace that may yet save us the pieces. As Bertrand Russell said, when intellectuals question if life is worth living while gardeners feel no doubt about it, it seems that intellectuals have something to learn from gardeners.

So have we all. A book I turned to this spring was *How to Enjoy Your Weeds,* by Audrey Wynne Hatfield of Hertfordshire, England. While outside the azaleas bloomed and the chickweed burgeoned, I found her as tolerant and hospitable a gardener as you could meet in May, a staunch admirer of weeds who respects their determination and greets them, somewhat selectively, with appropriate welcome. A lawn, she says, thrives on "companionable" weeds, such as clover (the clover leaf is a charm against witches) or camomile. Probably Sir Francis Drake played at bowls on a camomile green. The stinging nettle is as old as Pliny. About groundsel, a thriving weed, Nicholas Culpeper wrote, "This herb is Venus' mistress-piece." Unfortunately, as a love charm it seems to be sold now for the use of canaries and parakeets. As for mullein, for which the just claim is made that it protected Ulysses from being changed by Circe into a swine, in my countryside alone is enough mullein to save the whole human race.

If one remains skeptical, however, a good way to get rid of a weed is to eat it. Chickweed makes a nice salad or sandwich (or a poultice for carbuncles); the author highly recommends a day-lily fritter, sizzling hot, and lamb's quarters soup. These may be washed down with nettle beer or a good stout wild-carrot whiskey. For afternoon tea, there is the brewed dandelion or, if one wishes to offer guests something out of the ordinary, a *salade de pissenlit* (which takes courage).

Having learned to love a weed, I picked up a paperback called *Getting the Bugs Out of Organic Gardening* and read with profit the way to tell the good bugs from the bad. This is a fairly simple procedure, since there are only some 10,000 bad bugs; the rest are harmless. Doodlebugs are good. A ladybug, without doubt, is a treat to have around, whether she is a male or female ladybug—it makes no difference. She dines on potato beetles and she is a glutton for aphids. On the other hand, if you see an assassin bug eating a ladybug, that doesn't mean he is necessarily bad; he may have eaten her by mistake. Praying mantids will eat anything within reach, including each other. As this unruffled gardener says, you have to be philosophic about bugs, maintaining calm and avoiding panic when you come across a beetle in your beans. Killing everything in sight is not philosophic. Nobody ever said the world is pestproof, and one can learn to live gracefully in it. The first thing to do is not to feel trapped: you can get slugs drunk on beer. You can take a flour sifter and sift white flour about. You can invite in a few toads, lizards, and salamanders as resident pesticides, offering them a place in the sun and moon.

A benevolent book, *Digging It: How to Grow Things Naturally*, is by Diane Globus, a kind and merciful gardener from Vermont who quotes haiku and takes time out for transcendental meditation. She has much to say in praise of ladybugs. You buy them by the quart from Sears, Roebuck, though I don't find them listed in the spring catalogue. Since a single female aphid will produce a horrendous number of little aphids (enough to seize the world), the answer is clarion loud: ladybugs. If they fly away, that only means you haven't got enough aphids. Meanwhile, you can store the ladybugs in the refrigerator.

From her own pleasure in the good life ("Why not live surrounded by gardens?"), I am infected by her joy in her compost pile, the soul and essence of organic gardening. She explains, since this is a pile where nothing is a loss, how to become a scavenger and improve the essence by going on such expeditions as a visit to a bat cave, to a circus for peanut shells, to the sea for seaweed, to a bakery for eggshells, to a barbershop for hair. (Mr. White of Selborne used to sheer his mongrel dog Rover.)

Yet as I read on with absorption in her multiple affairs, I sense a danger in being swept by Miss Globus's zeal into excesses that, in the end, might leave no room in the garden for the gardener. I try to imagine following, with pardonable ambition, all of her friendly advice at once. I would now race over the garden scattering burlap bags with a bait of beer and molasses to catch the grasshoppers. I would build a nine-foot fence to keep out the deer, then sprinkle dried blood around (whose?) and human urine in case the deer jumped the fence. I would scare off the rabbits with Epsom salts or a pair of old sneakers; set out pans of moth-balls to outwit the moles; at night turn on a transistor radio in the cornpatch and string Christmas-tree lights overhead to flash on and off. I would spray my plants with a mist of garlic and cayenne pepper, not to destroy the bugs but to take away their appetite and hope they will die of starvation; douse my cabbages and fluttering cabbage butterflies with sour milk. At wit's end, I would let in a few Bantam hens, also any passing fox, snake, or skunk, since they love mice (and Bantam hens?). And I would take the ladybugs out of the refrigerator.

At last I understand why Thomas Jefferson of Monti-cello once advertised for a gardener who could play the French horn. I had always thought he wanted a man to en-tertain the company from time to time with a horn solo (Haydn's "Concerto for Horn in D Major"?). What Jef-ferson must have meant was somebody to blast off at the corn borers.

I love gardeners and their beautiful natures. They re-mind me of Bronson Alcott, who would eat only "aspir-ing" vegetables, those that grow up not down. *The New York Times Garden Book* is a rousing how-to book, crammed with advice fanciful and practical, proving gardeners to be not only inventive but romantic (like Wordsworth, "I was the Dreamer, they the Dream"). For instance, to start a wildflower garden, they tell you to haul in from woods and fields—provided woods and fields border the property—abundances of bluets, pink hepaticas, butter-fly weeds, meadow rue, trillium, wild ginger and the like. But if you insist on marsh marigolds, it helps to live in a swamp or bog. Artificial bogs are not successful.

These gracious gardeners will tell you even more than you knew you wanted to know—How to prune a rhododendron. How to espalier a firethorn (first you take a wall 35 feet high. Or perhaps one side of a skyscraper). How to grow strawberries in a nail keg or things in a waterjug. How to plant a wagon wheel (with herbs in the spokes). How to raise nut trees in the suburbs. How to landscape a penthouse. How to plant garlic among the roses to improve the smell (of which one I'm not sure). How to keep it up without flagging in all four seasons. "It is a good idea," says the editor, Joan Faust, "not to relax completely during January."

Gardeners are more than happy people—they are wits and optimists, by nature undaunted. It takes wit to find life worth living. It takes being undaunted to grow 25,000 species of orchids, or to talk to one's plants and allow the plants to talk back. But whether orchidaceous or earthy (like the resolute lady with an answer to every need: "Just invite in your friends and tell them to bring their spades"), they write books that cheer and certainly inebriate.

Virgil Says

Because he says to, not for pomp or whim,
Recite a loud ancestral hymn.
Beseech Arcturus his starlight
Upon your seedlings. Keep the morning rite
To Ceres, humble let it be.
And to ensure fertility
By pieties of heart and tongue,
For measure add a load of dung.
Petition first for rain, then bring
Three extra pots for watering.
Fright off the overweening birds
With clamor or with Latin words.
But lavish labor. Sweat! is his advice—
On this is Virgil most precise—
With which will piously concur
Any man or gardener.

Emily Dickinson at Home

Emily Dickinson could be tiresome, as when she sent down to a visitor whom she refused to see, "a single white clover laid on a spotless doily on a tiny silver tray." Or it might be two day lilies. That was being Miss Emily to a degree. Her girlish, demure ways kept into middle age, her refusal to leave the house, her wearing virginal white and letting no one see her save as a flutter light as a seraph past the parlor door, these Emilyisms seem not only melodramatic but downright peculiar. She was known in Amherst as "the myth."

Shortly after her thirtieth birthday, her retreat into seclusion (except from small children) became an obsession. Her isolation was complete. She never changed, content to hover out of sight, to hide upstairs from callers, fleeing when the doorbell rang. "To seek enchantment, one must always flee."

She advised her niece Martha, "Be sure, my dear, to live in vain. I wish I had." But what kind of advice was that? How does one go about living in vain? And why?

Without doubt, Emily could be a goose, a morbid spinster preoccupied with self, a withdrawn maiden lady given to wayward vanity, perhaps a bit touched in the head. When she died, by her own request her coffin was carried out the back door and through the barn. She tended to overplay the role even of recluse.

In her 1,775 poems she was all too often this Emily, coy and queer, with the same wilful singularity—in the "little girl" pieces addressing God as "Papa above" or calling herself "a little pussy catty." If she stained her apron with strawberries, God would certainly scold. When her Aunt Lavinia died, Emily sent a verse to her cousins,

> Mama never forgets her birds,
> Though in another tree.

She admitted that she loved being a child, with a soft childlike voice breathless over a squirrel or a bumblebee. She made a career of staying a child—in her delight in childish games and riddles, in the use of dashes and capital letters, exclamations and underlining, in the caprice and whimsy, the mystifications, the posturing.

> Papa above! Regard a Mouse
> O'erpowered by the Cat;
> Reserve within thy kingdom
> A "mansion" for the Rat!

But then, in a sudden splendor there is the revelation: the depth and power of her poet's mind, telling how much, how *much* she has missed:

> The missing all prevented me
> From missing minor things.
> If nothing larger than a world's
> Departure from a hinge
> Or sun's extinction, be observed
> 'Twas not so large that I
> Could lift my forehead from my work
> For curiosity.

Emily to Her Niece

Miss Emily, who knew better,
Told a lie in a friendly letter,
Advised her niece in a wistful strain:
"Be sure, my dear, to live in vain.
I wish I had."
Right there the meek Emily kept tongue in cheek.

Poet, with her quest of heaven,
Emily! whose mind was given
To stratagem in the earth's affair,
Tactic in the purpose here,
For whose surmise the day was brief
For the needful word, for the flower and leaf.

Were I the niece she lamented to,
I'd have written,
"Aunt, be yourself, dear. Do."

Aunt Mary Emerson in a Shroud

Emerson's Aunt Mary was a brilliant old maid, full of bounce, whose cheerful and favorite occupation was waiting for death. A small woman less than five feet tall and frolicsome, she was nonetheless a browbeater, a silencer of fools, a formidable female with an imperious temper and independent mind. When she traveled, she went in a shroud.

Aunt Mary reminded her loving nephew of Dr. Johnson, able to dominate and subdue a company as Johnson did, though she might command it as boldly, "Be still! I want to hear the men talk!" When Emerson read Dante, she reminded him of Dante. He called her a realist, but if so she was a mighty unpredictable one, who declared that Waldo need only fix his mind on the Christian faith and he could write *Paradise Lost* without the tiresome parts.

"Ah!" cried Aunt Mary, "what a poet would Byron have been, if he had been born and bred a Calvinist!"

Born herself before the American Revolution in 1774, she lived a solitary life to extreme old age and gloried in being poor, without yearning for wealth that she believed would spoil her, or for matrimony ("I knew I was not destined to please"). She was a sibyl, endowed, she admitted, with a fatal gift of penetration. Her eye went through and through you like a needle. She dismayed people by seeing too much, most of all their vanity. Irascible of temper, full of rebuke, disputatious, she was reputed to be able and willing to say more disagreeable things in twenty minutes than any other person alive ("I love to be a vessel of cumbersomeness to society"). Once when Emerson was trying to find a boardinghouse for her in Concord, where she wasn't welcome long, he told the landlady, "Miss Emerson is a constant east wind." She raised many a bluster, had many a falling-out. When Mrs. Thoreau called on her one afternoon wearing pink ribbons, Aunt Mary, who despised tact as only another name for lying, shut her eyes and kept them tight shut throughout the visit.

"Mrs. Thoreau, I don't know whether you have observed that my eyes are shut."
"Yes, Madam, I have observed it."
"Perhaps you would like to know the reasons?"
"Yes, I should."
"I don't like to see a person of your age guilty of such levity in her dress."

"Scorn trifles," Aunt Mary always said. "Fie on you!" she scolded in her role of public conscience. "Lift your aims! Do what you are afraid to do!" With her fiery, resolute nature, she looked forward to death with a perpetual lusty appetite and, dressed in her shroud, keeping a sharp eye on heaven, prepared impatiently for the final journey, that happy day of release. Emerson wrote:

For years she had her bed made in the form of a coffin. . . . She made up her shroud, and death still refusing to come, and thinking it a pity to let it lie idle, wore it as a night-gown, or a day-gown, nay, went out to ride in it, on horseback, in her mountain roads, until it was worn out. Then she had another made up, and as she never travelled without being provided for this dear and indispensable contingency, I believe she wore out a great many.

People remembered seeing her riding on horseback in her shroud through the streets of Concord, a red shawl flung around her thin shoulders. She must have looked like all four horsemen of the Apocalypse.

At times Aunt Mary grew discouraged waiting for an end too long delayed. She would rather be gibbeted, she said, than droop away at last. In her journal for 1833, with thirty years more to live, she wrote with regret, "I have given up, the last year or so, the hope of dying." But in 1835, laid low by an indisposition, again she took heart, trusting she might soon lie curled in her coffin, that her sickness might kindly open up "the cool, sweet grave." Not morbid but mortal, she reflected on her soon-to-be moldy bones and future most valuable companions, when "my lady worm" would banquet on her. "O dear worms."

After many annoying stays, Aunt Mary did manage to succumb, and briskly departed this life at the age of 88 years and 8 months. The greatly postponed event had a comic tinge, Emerson said. Her friends at the funeral— who well knew how tireless was her rehearsal of this moment; who while she lived used to wish her, like Cleopatra, joy of the worm—dared not look at each other for fear of laughing.

Aunt Mary and the Worm

Aunt Mary waited for the worm
With Christian fortitude, tenacity, and firm
Resolve. A practical solution
Braced her for her dissolution:
Her bed was fashioned like a coffin,
And shrouded in it, late and often,
She slept, at ease in that snug berth
Whose days were counted on the earth.
As if she knew the very number,
Aunt Mary lay at rest in placid slumber.

With solemn tread the years went by,
And though Aunt Mary failed to die
She lived expectant of her certain end,
So long that visitor or friend—
In timid effort to discuss
One topic not too frivolous
But fittingly bereft of hope
Within the confines of her conversational scope
And to Aunt Mary's taste—would squirm,
And joy would wish her of the worm.

Mrs. Trollope and the Spitters

Dickens thought Americans spit too much. So did Sydney Smith. So did Harriet Martineau, Captain Frederick Marryat, and Oscar Wilde. So did Mrs. Frances Trollope, mother of Anthony, who came to this country with three children in 1827 to open a department store in Cincinnati for the selling of fancy goods and knickknacks. The enterprise, known as "Trollope's Folly," failed and left her penniless. She stayed in America three years, then flounced home to write that two-volume work *Domestic Manners of the Americans,* loudly deploring our native habit of chewing tobacco and spitting on the carpet. Mrs. Trollope was fifty-two years old, a bossy woman, launched with this outraged book upon a literary career. In his *Autobiography,* Anthony apologized for his mother's ire. "The Americans were to her rough, uncouth, and vulgar,—and she told them so."

When she wrote, Andrew Jackson was President and his countrymen, she observed, were disgusting. "I do not like them," said Mrs. Trollope. "I do not like their principles, I do not like their manners, I do not like their opinions." They shoved. They twanged through their noses. The women called her Honey and shuddered at her "broken English." The men kept their hats on and feet up, drinking whiskey the while at tenpence a gallon. At a fashionable evening party in "hateful" Cincinnati, "The gentlemen spit, talk of elections and the price of produce, and spit again." At a performance of *Hamlet,* where they came in shirt sleeves, the spitting was incessant. A gentleman told her, "Shakespeare, madam, is obscene, and thank God we are sufficiently advanced to have found it out!"

150

From the gallery of Congress she studied the lawmakers with their hats on*—as Dickens viewed them ten years later, "The steady old chewers who missed the spittoon." Leaning closer, she saw their lips twisted out of shape as they spat "to an excess that decency forbids me to describe." Her name for them was George Washington Spitchew.

When the *Domestic Manners* became a best seller in both England and America (Southey and Wordsworth read and praised the book), it caused howls of resentment, indignation, and rage in this country, where for a time the author's name was a byword, a term of abuse. If a man happened to spit on the floor in a theater or put his feet up on the railing, he would hear catcalls of "A Trollope! A Trollope!" It served him right.

Sydney Smith never came to America. He read Mrs. Trollope in 1832 with amusement and enjoyed her picture of our manners: "Why should not the Americans be ridiculed if they are ridiculous?"

Yet he liked us in his friendly way and was only mildly disparaging, with two complaints against us—the spitting and the existence of slavery ("an atrocious crime"). In his essay "America," he said, "We are terribly afraid that some Americans spit upon the floor when that floor is covered by good carpets. Now all claims to civilization are suspended till this secretion is otherwise disposed of. No English gentleman has spit upon the floor since the Heptarchy."

Sydney Smith lived during George IV's regency and reign. I don't believe for a minute his claim about the man-

---

* Disraeli tilted his hat over his brow as he sat in the House of Commons. Peel pulled his hat over his eyes. The manners of Parliament in the '30s were the worst on record, with mooings, catcalls, and bellowings.   —From G. M. Young, *Portrait of an Age*

ners of the English. De Quincey, who was Smith's contemporary, told in an essay, "Conversation," published in *Tait's Magazine*, of gentlemen who took lessons in spitting from hackney coachmen, a guinea each for three lessons. The ultimate aim was to learn to spit around a corner. As late as the 1890's, a titled member of the Union Club in London was seen to spit into the milk jug at breakfast. He was requested to stop.

As a result of Sydney Smith's remarks, taken as assault, the Americans abused him dreadfully. "They call me Xantippe. They might at least have known my sex."

With Mrs. Trollope and her gibes, Americans felt an increased suspicion of the visiting English. Before her arrival they had grown touchy under years of rebuke, and at least one American, James Paulding, had answered back. In 1825, *John Bull in America* appeared, an outrageous caricature of the British traveler with a nose like a potato who, enlightened by the savage attacks on us in the London *Quarterly Review*, came to find a barbarous race given to "bundling, gouging, drinking, spitting." James Fenimore Cooper went as a visitor to England in 1828 and met with such chilling insolence and sneers that he recoiled with hurt feelings in a book, *Gleanings*. He found himself insulted even by gentle Joanna Baillie, who when she met him shivered in horror: "But then, your rattlesnakes!"

In 1829, Captain Basil Hall, an English naval officer, had published *Travels in America* with remarks so upsetting to us (causing war whoops and "a sort of moral earthquake," said Mrs. Trollope) that the *American Quarterly Review* claimed the British government had commissioned him to write the book to keep the English people from admiring our country and envying our peaceful and harmonious ways.

So when Harriet Martineau crossed the Atlantic—a deaf maiden lady of thirty-two, a strict Unitarian in bonnet and shawl carrying an ear trumpet—a friend asked as she set sail, "Have you no misgivings?" "None," said Harriet Martineau.

She stayed two years, accepted as gospel all she thought she heard, and in 1837 published her finds in *Society in America* and in 1838 *Retrospect of Western Travel*, each in three volumes. Both books carried an air of calm yet severe reproof and a strong plea for reform, especially of education in our Sunday schools. (A Sunday-school teacher asked a child, "In what state was mankind left after the fall?" The child replied, "In the state of Vermont.") Her didactic work, like Mrs. Trollope's, was regarded as slanderous, a cruel breach of hospitality. She had fed at our tables and criticized our food ("The dish from which I ate was, according to some, mutton; to others, pork; my own idea is that it was dog"). She was accused of spying.

Though Miss Martineau protested she found Americans amiable and hospitable, of a sweetness of temper "which is diffused like sunshine over the land," she found them also plunged, women and men, into a living hell of intemperance (to her knowledge, seven or eight such cases existed in the higher classes of society in one city). She deplored our moral timidity, so unlike her own strength. She was annoyed by our rocking chairs.

As for the chewing of tobacco and its fearful consequences: "I will say nothing but that the practice is at too bad a pass to leave hope that anything that could be said in books would work a cure. If the floors of boarding-houses and the decks of steamboats and the carpets of the Capitol do not sicken the Americans into a reform, if the warnings of physicians are of no avail, what remains to be said? I dismiss the nauseous subject."

Captain Frederick Marryat arrived in 1837 and stayed eighteen months, a tactless and blundering guest, an insolent English novelist who behaved so rudely he was threatened by a lynch mob and hanged in effigy at least twice. In Detroit a furious crowd gathered to burn his books and shout execrations at him. He was entertained by Henry Clay, whom he was reported, inaccurately, to have insulted in his own house.

Like Mrs. Trollope's, Marryat's name became a household word, and when he published his *Diary in America* it gave offense equal to hers for reviling our bumptious deportment. "They had no right to insult and annoy me in the manner they did, from nearly one end of the Union to the other."

"But why do they get so confoundedly drunk?" he asked. Why do they always shake hands? Why do they constantly chew tobacco? So prevalent was the habit of chewing, he wrote, that the horrid article was sold in the smart shops and young ladies carried it in their workboxes for their swains. Elegant young men kept wads of it in their silk waistcoats and stuffed it in their cheeks. America was a sideshow to Marryat, a preposterous collection of freaks and upstarts.

Dickens sailed for America in January, 1842, made his own considerable contribution to Anglo-American discord, and returned home thankfully in June. His *American Notes* aroused righteous anger in this country for his shocking manners in writing about our own. His new novel *Martin Chuzzlewit*, in which Martin goes to America and meets with fraud and ill-treatment, caused understandable hysteria among the critics, who, said Dickens, wrote about the book as if they were "stark, staring, raving mad." Such words as his, as Mrs. Gamp would say, "lambs could not forgive . . . nor worms forget."

Dickens' satire was heaviest against the spitters, through his character the Honourable Elijah Pogram, Member of Congress, ruminating over his tobacco-plug like a cow; and Mr. Hannibal Chollop, windbag, laboring under the "not uncommon delusion that for a free and enlightened citizen of the United States to convert another man's house into a spittoon for two or three hours together was a delicate attention, full of interest and politeness, of which nobody could ever tire."

"I re-quire, sir," said Hannibal, "two foot clear in a circ'lar di-rection, and can engage myself toe keep within it. I *have* gone ten foot, in a circ'lar di-rection; but that was for a wager."

Before his sailing to our shores, Lady Holland had asked him, "Why cannot you go down to Bristol and see some of the third and fourth class people there and they'll do just as well?" But at first, favorably impressed by America and its throngs to welcome him, Dickens tended to be laudatory after two triumphant weeks of being lionized in Boston.

Then all went wrong, the impression reversed itself. He became aware of crudity and impertinence when his privacy was intruded upon, when dreadful pests talked of dollars and politics, the mobs mauled him, the press derided him. Americans were greedy and vulgar—as they found him to be with his ringlets and crimson waistcoats, his public talk of the money he was being cheated out of.

Most intolerable (besides slavery, and the lack of copyright to protect his books) was the spitting. In a letter to his friend Maclise he wrote, "I have twice seen gentlemen at evening parties in New York, turn aside when they were not engaged in conversation, and spit upon the drawing-room carpet."

President John Tyler had a brass spittoon, more elegantly called a cuspidor, in his office. (Charles Mackay, in 1859, suggested it become our national emblem instead of the eagle.) In the Congress of Daniel Webster, John Quincy Adams, Clay, Calhoun, Dickens watched men chewing such mighty quids that their faces looked swollen. On a Mississippi riverboat, Dickens' uneasy wife, Kate, had her dress covered with flying tobacco spittle carried by the wind from a man in the front seat. She spent most of the visit in tears and mute despair.

If Dickens was indignant, so were the Americans. It took years of wrath before either could forgive the other's failure in courtesy. Not until twenty-five years later, after the Civil War, when Dickens returned in 1867 for his second American tour did he find us passably civilized and, this time, admiring.

Oscar Wilde materialized in New York in January, 1882, on the S.S. *Arizona* from Liverpool, wearing a bottle-green, fur-lined coat, sealskin cap, yellow kid gloves, his long chestnut hair to his shoulders, and made his famous opening remark when asked if he had anything to declare: "Nothing but my genius." That set the tone.

The Gilbert and Sullivan opera *Patience* had appeared with some success on the New York stage that September, and D'Oyly Carte was responsible for bringing Wilde over as an added attraction—Bunthorne in the flesh. America already knew about this too utterly utter young man who walked down Picadilly with a poppy or a lily in his medieval hand.

After languidly attending a performance of *Patience* on January 6, on January 9 at Chickering Hall in New York Wilde delivered his first lecture, wearing black velvet knee breeches, black silk stockings, white waistcoat, Byronic collar, white tie and gloves, his hair parted in the middle and curled. He chose to speak on the "English Renaissance," about which the audience knew little and cared less. In spite of his fame as an oddity, they grew restive, then bored, then incredulous.

Undaunted, he persevered in seventy towns during his lecture tour, a natural exhibitionist with a flair for antagonizing Americans by his extraordinary mannerisms, his drawl, his droop, his swaying walk, his high-flown words on beauty and the soul, his pose hand on hip as an aesthetic. He was appearing as a work of art.

While at Philadelphia, he took time to visit Walt Whitman in Camden, New Jersey, and drink with him some homemade elderberry wine. They warmed to each other, Whitman at sixty-three after a paralytic stroke, Wilde at twenty-eight though he gave his age as twenty-six. "There is something so Greek and sane about his poetry," he observed of his host and sat on a little stool at Whitman's feet.

"I should like to call you Oscar," said Walt Whitman.

"I like that so much," said Oscar, laying a hand on Whitman's knee.

From there he traveled to Rochester, Buffalo, and Niagara Falls (which like the Atlantic Ocean disappointed him, "I am not exactly pleased with the Atlantic"), and

the natives went on laughing, calling him the "ass-thete."
He tried a new subject for his talks, "Interior and Exterior
Decoration of Houses," and in Cleveland they said, "Remember that Cleveland's politeness is on trial." In Du-
buque, Iowa, most of the seats were empty for his performance. He was totally defeated in Texas. At St. Paul,
Omaha, Cheyenne, they noted with laughter the lavish fur
robe he carried with him to hide the hideous sofas in hotel
rooms; they split their sides at his flowing locks, his English
accent. They said he wore a wig. They said he looked like
George Eliot. They waved sunflowers and calla lilies in his
face to mock him. His American tour was a failure. In
general we treated him as a thoroughly bad joke.

But Oscar Wilde was never one to be silenced by attack. "The cities of America are inexpressably tedious," he
said, full of bustle and bores. He told the people of Salt
Lake City their Mormon Tabernacle had the shape of a
soup kettle. When he turned up at the mining camp in
Leadville, Colorado, he praised the miners as "the only
well-dressed men I have seen in America." The press denounced him for making rude and uncomplimentary remarks.

As always, he had the last word. On his return to England, having sailed on December 27, Oscar Wilde summed
up the whole misadventure in one of his best witticisms:
"In America, life is one long expectoration."

Mrs. Trollope in America

Mrs. Trollope took a doleful view
Of us, in 1832,
Whose native latitude she knew.

And every time a gentleman spit,
Not being edified a whit,
She made a plaintive note of it.

Her agitation grew so great,
At times she seemed to lie in wait
For somebody to expectorate.

But we, in 1832,
Took a more broad, dispassionate view,
And spit whenever we wanted to.

Beautiful Lofty Courtesans

Landor's 150 *Imaginary Conversations* bore me. He is tedious. He is dull. He is improbable. In two talks between "Aesop and Rhodope," he is prudish, inventing a mawkish tale of Rhodope's being sold into slavery by a loving father to save her from starvation. She was a fellow slave with Aesop at Samos, who addresses her as "my little maiden." "Expect no love from me," says Aesop.

What Landor carefully avoided saying is that Rhodope became a beautiful courtesan who sold her love and grew wealthy. She was the Greek Cinderella—a far better fairy tale than Landor's—who lost a sandal one day while bathing, and, according to Aelian, Fortune gave her a reward suitable not to her mind but to her beauty. An eagle flew off with the sandal and dropped it in the lap of the Pharaoh of Egypt. He hurried to seek out Rhodope and marry her. Some say she afterward erected one of the pyramids. Not so, says Herodotus: as a memorial to herself, she sent a lot of iron ox-spits to Delphi.

The courtesans I'm partial to were Greek, the hetaerae, whose lives richly illustrated the moral of beauty rewarded. Phryne, mistress of Praxiteles, stood as a radiant gold statue in the Temple of Apollo at Delphi. She offered to rebuild Thebes at her own expense after Alexander destroyed it but was refused. For once she asked too much—the carving of a prostitute's name as benefactor. Galen told how ravishing she was. At a party, in a game of follow-the-leader Phryne led off by washing her face in a bowl of water. The other women had to reveal their true faces and were disgraced, a low ruse of Phryne's. When she was accused in Athens of impiety (for which the penalty was

160

death), the orator Hyperides, also her lover, defended her in the courtroom by throwing open her robe and showing the whiteness of her breasts. The judges hastily freed her, not daring to condemn the goddess of love herself, though a decree was made "that hereafter no orator should endeavor to excite pity on behalf of anyone."

Laïs, mistress of Alcibiades, came high-priced at Corinth and men called her greedy, she who gave herself without cost to Diogenes. This union of body and mind must have appealed to her, since in general she mocked philosophers as appearing at her door with the same lusts as other men. Laïs (called Axinē—the axe—because of her cruel ways) was a temperamental beauty, witty too. Artists used to come to Corinth to copy her perfect breasts. When the sculptor Myron was refused her bed, he put on a scarlet robe and a golden girdle, rouged his cheeks, perfumed himself, dyed his white hair brown and returned. "Fool," said Laïs, "to ask what I refused yesterday to thy father." Aristippus, on the other hand, enjoyed her body but announced with small thanks, "I have Laïs, not she me."

The real lady among them, Aspasia, was the mistress of Pericles. Plutarch praises the love Pericles felt for her, so connubial a rapture that every day as he went out and returned from the marketplace he kissed her, his lifelong love after he divorced his wife and found her another husband. Aspasia had a small foot, silvery voice, golden hair, and such intellect that those who frequented her company would bring their wives along for self-improvement just to listen to her. Socrates, a steady caller, was among her scholars when she first came to Athens and taught eloquence. So was Pericles, who became an orator of thundering rhetoric at her feet. She is given some credit by Aristophanes for causing the Peloponnesian War.

Yet she was called a harlot, accused of bringing prostitutes to Athens and keeping them in her house. She too was tried for impiety and corrupting the morals of upright citizens. By the oratory of a weeping Pericles she was set free.

Prudish old Walter Savage Landor, though, ruined the story of this splendid love affair by writing *Pericles and Aspasia*, 1836, a two-volume collection of imaginary letters, in which he made no attempt to be accurate, amorous, or even inventive. "In writing my *Pericles and Aspasia*," he boasted, "I had no books to consult. The characters, thoughts, and actions, all are fictions." Then he added a twenty-five-page essay on English politics.

Demosthenes said every man requires, besides his wife, at least two mistresses. Any one of these beautiful lofty girls would seem to be world enough. (Why were the Greeks supposed to have been given to homosexual practices when they spent all their spare time with *women?*) Or was Thaïs of Athens the loveliest courtesan of antiquity? —the mistress of Alexander the Great, who accompanied him into Asia, and according to Plutarch had such power over him that when she rose at a banquet in the stately palace of Xerxes and swore she would like to reduce the place to ashes with her own hands, drunken Alexander wearing a chaplet of flowers and carrying a lighted torch set about burning Persepolis to please her.

The poets gave Thaïs immortality by their praise. Menander's lauds of her physical allure caused her to be named Menandrea. Dryden's ode "Alexander's Feast" inspired him to his most lyric heights, the story of the royal feast following the conquest of Persia, when the victorious Alexander sat on his imperial throne, the whole world at his feet, and

> The lovely Thaïs by his side
> Sate like a blooming Eastern bride,
> In flower of youth and beauty's pride.
>   Happy, happy, happy pair!
>   None but the brave,
>   None but the brave,
>   None but the brave deserves the fair.

Twice in his manuscript, Dryden managed to confuse Thaïs with Laïs (one courtesan is like another) and so had to ask his printer, Tonson, to remember to change the name, with the excuse: "those two Ladyes were Contemporaryes, wch caused that small mistake."

In the Inferno, Thaïs the whore appears in the eighth circle of Hell, immersed in excrement.

Dr. Johnson and Bet Flint

Dr. Johnson loved to talk about Bet Flint, a woman of the town, habitually a slut and a drunkard, occasionally a thief and a harlot.

He made her acquaintance in London when Bet wrote her autobiography in verse, calling herself Cassandra, and brought it to Dr. Johnson for criticism, hoping he would provide a Preface to it. It began:

> When Nature first ordain'd my birth,
> A diminutive I was born on earth:
> And then I came from a dark abode,
> Into a gay and gaudy world.

Dr. Johnson gave her a half-crown instead; but Bet had a fine spirit and he laughed to remember her comical ways. Once she advertised for a husband with no success, since (she told Dr. Johnson) no man aspired to her. Somehow she found genteel lodgings, to avoid mixing in low company, and bought a harpsichord on which she tried to play with a ladylike air and languid gestures but could only drum. She had a footboy to walk before her chair. With these proofs of gentility she was well content.

In 1781 when Dr. Johnson was seventy-two, still thinking fondly of Bet Flint, he gave Boswell a highly entertaining account of how she had stolen a quilt or counterpane, been arrested, tried at Old Bailey, and acquitted by a Chief Justice "who loved a wench." The incident had happened twenty-three years before, in 1758 (according to the *Sessional Reports of the Old Bailey Trials*, Bet had stolen from her landlord not only the counterpane but five other articles), yet she was as fresh in his mind as yesterday and dear to him still.

When he told the same story to Mrs. Thrale and Fanny Burney, "I have known all the wits," declared Dr. Johnson to those surprised listeners, "from Mrs. Montague down to Bet Flint."

"Bet Flint!" cried Mrs. Thrale. "Pray, who is she?"

"Oh, a fine character, madam."

Bet Flint

August, 1778. "Bet Flint!" cried
Mrs. Thrale. "Pray, who is she?

Bet was a trollop. As Dr. Johnson put it
(Who was better informed than I), she was a slut,
A wench of easy virtue, a London harlot,
A common thief besides and a drunkard. But
"Oh, a fine character, madam," said Dr. Johnson,
Who loved Bet Flint, not for her morals, no,
Certainly not for her person—a man untempted—
Nor for her intellect. For something, though,
He valued her: perhaps her unquenchable spirit,
The time she stole a quilt and was sent to jail,
Arriving in style with footboy and sedan chair—
"Oh, I loved Bet Flint!" he confessed to Mrs. Thrale.
The Justice loved her too and acquitted her,
And she laughed "So the quilt is mine," with not one hint
Of remorse or shame or penitence or contrition,
And made a petticoat of it. I love Bet Flint.

David Garrick, Actor of Actors

All the reports agree that David Garrick was a great actor, some say the greatest of all time. William Cooke, a contemporary, tells in *Memoirs of Macklin* of a grocer from Lichfield who came to visit London with a letter of introduction to Garrick from his brother, Peter Garrick. The grocer went first to a play at the Drury Lane, where he saw the actor as Abel Drugger, the sneaky tobacconist in *The Alchemist*. When he returned to Lichfield without paying his call, he was still shaken. He told Peter Garrick:

"I saw enough of him on the stage. He may be rich, as I dare say any man who lives like him must be. But by God! though he is your brother, Mr. Garrick, he is one of the shabbiest, meanest, most pitiful hounds I ever saw in the whole course of my life."

Fanny Burney adored the charmer Garrick, a close friend of her family. In her Diary she shudders at him as Abel Drugger, a horrid sly little lout, a fellow in a dirty wig and smock, a simpleton with a vacant stare. "Never could I have imagined such a metamorphose as I saw; the extreme meanness, the vulgarity, the low wit, the vacancy of countenance, the appearance of *unlicked nature* in all his motions. In short, never was character as well entered into, yet so opposite to his own."

In his role of Richard III, says Miss Burney, "Garrick was sublimely horrible!" Her father exclaimed, "Even the skirts of his coat acted." Dr. Johnson told Mrs. Thrale of his success as the hunchback Richard (which with Abel Drugger and the valet Sharp in his own farce, *The Lying Valet*, gave Garrick his tremendous reputation in the

1740's). After seeing him as Richard, a lady sent proposals of marriage, mentioning her large fortune and noble birth. Garrick encouraged her through a female friend who acted as go-between, but abruptly the negotiations were broken off. Two years passed. One day Garrick, meeting the go-between on the street, begged for an explanation. She hesitated, then told him:

"Well Sir, the truth is the best excuse. I will tell it you: my friend fell in love with you playing Richard, but seeing you since in the character of the lying valet, you looked so —*shabby* (pardon me, Sir) that it cured her of her passion."

Garrick went often to Old Bailey to memorize the anguished faces of men and women on trial for their lives. To play Lear, he studied a madman—one who had been driven violently insane by a personal tragedy, when he killed his two-year-old daughter by accidentally dropping her out of an upper window. On seeing his child's crushed body lying on the pavement below, the frantic father went out of his mind. He continued to live in his house in Leman Street with two keepers, where he passed his lunatic days at the same window reinacting the scene, letting his child slip again through his hands, then shrieking and screaming in terror. Garrick went several times to watch the performance. Afterward he would act it out for his friends.

"There it was that I learned to imitate madness," he said. "I copied nature, and to that owed my success in King Lear."

He managed as Lear to petrify his audience with his howling curses, dissolve it in tears (Boswell: "I was fully moved, and I shed abundance of tears"), and by freely rewriting Shakespeare send it away happy with both Cordelia and Lear alive, the king hale at the end, back on his throne.

If Garrick copied nature, he had a bag of clever tricks besides, even to a well-practiced death rattle that he liked to prolong. In the death scenes, which he improvised and extended—giving Macbeth a dying speech, allowing Romeo to expire at considerable length—he grew haggard before one's eyes. His start of terror on seeing the Ghost in *Hamlet* was a supreme moment on the stage. Fielding immortalized it in *Tom Jones,* where at a London performance Partridge, convinced the ghost is real, calls Garrick no actor at all since any man so confronted would behave in the same way.

"*He* the best player!" says Partridge with a sneer. "Why I could act as well as he myself. I am sure if I had seen a ghost, I should have looked in the very same manner and done as well as he did."

When Garrick cried out in *Macbeth,* "There's blood upon thy face," his piercing look was so frightening that the actor playing a murderer gave a start, put his hand to his face, and exclaimed, "Is there, by God?"

And each time the audience stamped and applauded, till Mrs. Clive, his envious leading lady, said of Garrick: "Damn him! I believe he could act a gridiron."

Oliver Goldsmith, however, in his poem "Retaliation" saw his old friend in a less brilliant light—as a man who couldn't stop acting and always gave his showiest performances offstage:

> On the stage he was natural, simple, affecting:
> 'Twas only that when he was off he was acting.

The Countess of Pembroke's Book

She had an excellent wit, good breeding, and reddish-yellow hair. She knew Latin, Greek, and Hebrew. John Aubrey, gossiping about her many lovers, said she was lusty and salacious. She liked to peep out through a hole to watch the stallions leap on the mares in the spring, then encourage her lovers in the same spring rites. Lust and wit go hand in hand, I think, but that is beside the point. The Countess of Pembroke loved books. She used to pin quotations from them to her bedroom furniture to memorize while dressing.

Her older brother Philip (also her lover, if one can believe John Aubrey, and one cannot. "I have heard old gentlemen say that they lay together") began his tale of pastoral romance at her country house Wilton at her request, probably in 1580 if not before, since he spent much of that year with her.

"You desired me to do it," he said, "and your desire to my heart is an absolute commandment."

All summer long she sat by his side in the garden as he wrote to beguile the time, "only for you, only to you," Mary Sidney's book, the Countess of Pembroke's *Arcadia*. "Here now have you (most dear, and most worthy to be most dear, lady) this idle work of mine." In the enchanted world of Arcadia, the way to live forever after was to be in love. Wilton became his Arcadia, where Mary was.

He meant it only for her because of the love between them. Aubrey says Philip Sidney was downright beautiful, much resembling his undeniably beautiful sister, though his hair was darker than hers, of dark amber color. Spenser

said Sidney looked like his sister "in a divine resem-
blance." On the other hand, Ben Jonson told Drummond
at Hawthornden, "Sir P. Sidney was no pleasant man in
countenance, his face being spoiled with pimples, and of
high blood and long." Here I take old Aubrey's word for it.

Like those notorious Arcadian poets Virgil and Milton,
Sidney never in his life saw the place. He neither knew nor
visited the real Arcadia, though the scene is laid there. The
Arcadia begins with shepherds and eclogues, the usual
conventions of bucolic bliss. It gives an idealized, highly
inaccurate picture of emerald grass, meadows of bright
flowers, pretty lambs, well-tuned birds including the nightingale, stately trees in a continual spring, a shepherd boy
piping, a young shepherdess knitting "and withall singing."

Sidney called it a "toyfull book," a trifle that he never
bothered to finish. Read it and laugh, he told his sister,
blame not its follies, continue to love the writer who does
exceedingly love you. Sometime later he picked up the
manuscript and fussed with it, undertaking an enlargement
to give the meandering artificial plot and riotous invention
more form and unity. But it was hardly worth the trouble.
He broke off, as if impatient, in the middle of a sentence.

She must have loved it as it was, the first *Arcadia,* with
its sonnets written to her, its love songs. She must have got
it by heart, pinning the words to her pincushion or over
her mirror to read while she gazed at herself and brushed
her reddish-yellow hair:

> My true love hath my heart, and I have his,
> By just exchange one for the other given:
> I hold his dear, and mine he cannot miss,
> There never was a better bargain driven.

As Sidney lay dying at thirty-two, after a musket ball shattered his thigh at Zutphen, he asked to have the manuscript of the *Arcadia* suppressed and burned to ashes, "lest," wrote his friend Fulke Greville afterward, "it prove an incentive to amorous passions." Said Aubrey: "He made it young, and Diying desired his folies might be burnt." Instead of words, he would leave his best jewel beset with diamonds to Mary. But his sister chose to disobey him. It was her name on his lips as he died. It was her book he left behind. She kept alive the gift he had given her.

Hadn't they, after all, conceived it together by the love between them?

The Accidents of John Aubrey

For a happy man, John Aubrey was the unluckiest I've met in my life. From the day of his birth, he had a talent for mishaps, mortifications, calamities, disasters, and plain trouble that marked him star-crossed. Miscellaneous and random misfortunes rained upon him, a man whose "affaires ran kim kam; nothing tooke effect." He was accident prone to such a degree that, recognizing the fact, he made a memorandum called "Accidents of John Aubrey" that was found preserved among his papers after his death. Though *accidents* as an astrological term can mean notable events (and Aubrey was a firm believer in astrology, portents, omens, apparitions, visions, voices, and second sight), one look at his memorandum assures the skeptic that accidents must be what he meant—afflictive and unfortunate happenings, or pure bad luck.

Yet John Aubrey was a happy man, much tumbled by fate. He loved existence and easily forgave its merciless attacks, which appear to have caused him only temporary chagrin. He stayed glad and affectionate, one whose chief virtue he said himself was gratitude. His delightful collection of *Brief Lives* was made over a period of twenty-five years (1670–1696) after life had dealt him its worst blow and left him penniless, indigent, a hanger-on completely dependent on the hospitality of friends. He wrote as a relaxed and amused observer some 426 lives, candid accounts of his contemporaries and of interesting people who lived in the century before—Shakespeare, Ben Jonson, Raleigh, Bacon. These he left in manuscript as haphazard and incomplete notes, of which only 134 have been found in any shape to be publishable.

Aubrey's method was simple: he would rise at dawn in the house of some friend who had taken him in and, while his host slept off the night's conviviality, snatch up his note-book to jot down anything he remembered about whoever came to mind. He left blanks for dates, stuck in a piece of information or hearsay as it occurred to him, and wrote any private matter he pleased. In between times he whipped about asking old people what they recalled, collecting material in so daft a fashion that Anthony Wood predicted he would break his neck one day running hither and yon. But then Wood was peevish and mean enough to call him "magotieheaded," shiftless and a little crazed.

As a result of tireless curiosity, Aubrey dealt in particulars of a most engaging sort (sometimes inaccurate, says his editor, Mr. Lawson Dick, but never untruthful)—the kind of gossip anyone loves to hear:

Of Sir Francis Bacon: "He had a delicate, lively, hazel eie; Dr. Harvey tolde me it was like the Eie of a viper."

Of Richard Corbet, bishop: "His conversation was extreme pleasant. Dr. Stubbins was one of his Cronies; he was a jolly fatt Dr. and a very good house-keeper; parson in Oxfordshire. As Dr. Corbet and he were riding in Lob Lane in wett weather ('tis an extraordinary deepe, dirty lane) the coach fell; and Dr. Corbet sayd that Dr. Stubbins was up to his elbowes in mud, he was up to his elbowes in Stubbins."

Of Sir William Harvey: "He bid me goe to the Fountain head, and read Aristotle, Cicero, Avicenna, and did call the Neoteriques [modern writers] shitt-breeches. . . . He was wont to say that man was but a great, mischievous Baboon."

Of Sir Jonas Moore, mathematician: "Sciatica: he cured it by boyling his Buttock."

Of Sir Walter Raleigh: "He loved a wench well; and one time getting up one of the Mayds of Honour up against a tree in a Wood ('twas his first Lady) who seemed at first boarding to be something fearfull of her Honour, and modest, she cryed, sweet Sir Walter, what doe you me ask? Will you undoe me? Nay, sweet Sir Walter! Sweet Sir Walter! Sir Walter! At last, as the danger and the pleasure at the same time grew higher, she cryed in the extasey, Swisser Swatter Swisser Swatter."

Of William Prynne, Puritan sectarian writer: "His manner of Studie was thus: he wore a long quilt cap, which came 2 or 3, at least, inches over his eies, which served him as an Umbrella to defend his Eies from the light. About every three houres his man was to bring him a roll and a pott of Ale to refocillate his waster spirits."

John Aubrey was born at sunrise in Wiltshire, March 12, 1626, "very weak and like to Dye," christened before morning prayer lest he do so. "I think I have heard my mother say I had an Ague shortly after I was born."

1629.   About three or four years old I had a grievous ague, I can remember it. I got not health till eleven or twelve, but had sickness of Vomiting for 12 hours every fortnight for years, then it came monthly then quarterly & then half yearly, the last was in June 1642. This sickness nipt my strength in the bud.

1633.   At eight years old I had an issue (naturall) in the coronal sutor of my head, which continued running till 21. [He lived as a child in "eremitical solitude" and loneliness.]

1634.   October, I had a violent fevor, it was like to have carried me off; 'twas the most dangerous sickness that ever I had.

As a schoolboy, Aubrey suffered from "the belly-ake; paine in the side." He had a stammer, he was mocked and abused. Excessive whipping "did make a convulsive pain in my tender braine, which doubtless did doe me a great deal of hurt."

On entering Trinity College, Oxford, at sixteen, he soon caught the smallpox and was forced to return home, where for the next three years he lived "a sad life" in the country, on bad terms with his father, who so disapproved of book-learning that Aubrey was forced to study on horse-back or in the privy. Admitted to the Middle Temple in London, he had no time to learn law before being called home by his father's illness and financial distress. With his father's death, though heir to a large fortune Aubrey was plunged into lawsuits for the next fifteen years, losing estate after estate till he had managed to forfeit all he pos-sessed. Meanwhile, the accidents waxed and multiplied.

1652.   Truly nothing; only umbrages.

1655.   (I think) June 14. I had a fall at Epsam & brake one of my ribbes, and was afraid it might cause an apostumation.

1656.   This yeare and the last was a strange yeare to me. Several love and lawe suites. . . . Decem ♀ morb. [*Veneris morbus*, the planetary sign of Venus].

1659.   March or April like to break my neck in Ely Minster; and the next day, riding a gallop there my horse tumbled over and over; and yet I thank God no hurt.

1664.   June 11 landed at Calais, in August following had a terrible fit of the spleen and piles at Orleans.

1664 or 1665.   Munday after Christmas was in danger to be spoiled by my horse; and the same day received *laesio in testiculo*, which was like to have been fatal.

1665. November 1. I made my first address (in an ill hour) to Joane Sumner.

Unlucky in everything else, John Aubrey was born to be unlucky in love. After wooing three women, he gave up and tried no more to marry. Mrs. M. Wiseman, "that incomparable good conditioned gentlewoman with whom at first sight I was in love," married someone else. Katherine Ryves "with whom I was to marry" fell sick and died. In an evil hour in 1666, he took out a license to wed Joan Sumner, having promised to settle his lands on her that were already mortgaged, and found himself entangled in three years of squabble and litigation when she accused him of conspiring to defraud her.

1666. This yeare all my business and affaires ran kim kam, nothing tooke effect, as if I had been under an ill tongue. Treacheries and enmities in abundance against me.

1667. December—Arrested in Chancery Lane at Mrs. Sumner's suite.

1668. July 6. was arrested by Peter Gale's malicious contrivance.

1669. March 5 was my triall at Winton from eight to nine. The Judge being exceedingly made against me by my Lady Hungerford. . . .

1669 and 1670. I sold all my Estate in Wilts. From 1670 to this very day (I thank God) I have enjoyed a happy delitescency.

Aubrey was forty-five when his ruin was complete. To avoid imprisonment for debt, he fled, constantly changing his London lodgings. He considered entering a monastery or emigrating to America. He sold his last possessions, his

beloved books. What he had left was not even resentment
—only a "happy delitescency." Unnettled and unscathed he
became an indigent wanderer, sponging on his friends, who
found him very good company. ("I had never quiett, nor
anything of happiness till divested of all.") With the Earl
of Thanet he was delitescent "neer a yeare." Sir Christopher Wren and Mr. Thomas Hobbes looked after him.
Edmund Wyld of Glasley Hall "tooke me in his armes."

And the accidents persisted:

1671.   Danger of Arrests.

1677.   Latter end of June an impostume brake in my
head (about 50 years of impostume in head). St.
John's night 1673 in danger of being run through
with a sword by a young templer at M. Burges' chamber in the Middle Temple.

I was in danger of being killed by William Earl of
Pembroke then Lord Herbert at the election of Sir
William Salkeld for New Sarum. I have been in
danger of being drowned twice.

The year that I lay at M. Neve's (for a short time)
I was in great danger of being killed by a drunkard
in the Street of Grays Inn Gate by a Gentleman whom
I never saw before but (*Deo gratias*) one of his
companions hindred his thrust.

Even at life's end, twenty years later, Aubrey's doom-
ful fate pursued him. A late tribulation occurred on
March 20, 1693, when at 11:00 P.M. he was robbed and
received fifteen wounds in the head. Then "surpriz'd by
age," he died and, at the Oxford he had always loved, was
buried in an unmarked grave in the Church of St. Mary
Magdalen. The entry of his burial says only this:

1697.   John Aubery a stranger was Buryed Jun. 7th.

Sydney Smith, a Nice Person

Sydney Smith was a nice person. Since he himself defined what a nice person is, it is plain to see that the definition fits:

A nice person is neither too tall nor too short, looks clean
and cheerful, has no prominent feature, makes no difficulties,
is never misplaced, sits bodkin [wedged between two others],
is never foolishly affronted, and is void of affectations . . . .

A nice person is clear of little, trumpery passions, acknowl-
edges superiority, delights in talent, shelters humility, pardons
adversity, forgives deficiency, respects all men's rights, never
stops the bottle, is never long and never wrong, always knows
the day of the month, the name of every body at table, and
never gives pain to any human being . . . .

A nice person never knocks over wine or melted butter, does
not tread upon the dog's foot, or molest the family cat, eats
soup without noise, laughs in the right place, and has a watch-
ful and attentive eye.

To my taste, Sydney Smith is one of the nicest persons
who ever lived. Of the men I wish I had known—Montaigne, Sir Thomas More, Mr. White of Selborne—he is
of their gracious company. Like More, he was mighty
facetious. Like Montaigne he was scandalously serene. Unlike Gilbert White he had no relish for the country ("It
is a kind of healthy grave"), but, finding no alternative,
spent twenty years on a three-hundred-acre farm in Yorkshire dependably cheerful, in love with his wife, never
bored, happy and at peace. He fitted two of his donkeys
with antlers to look like deer. He thanked God who had
made him poor that he had made him merry. He wrote to

179

Lady Holland: "If my lot be to crawl, I will crawl contentedly; if to fly, I will fly with alacrity; but as long as I can possibly avoid it I will never be unhappy."

By his definition, a nice person is not called upon to be amusing. It is an added attraction. Charles Greville in his *Diary* says if there was a fault in Sydney Smith it was that he was too amusing. People expected to die laughing when he spoke and nearly did. Seldom could they recall afterward what made them laugh, only that they panted and cried for mercy. With a strong sense of the ridiculous, he was funny, hilarious, a Falstaff (never a buffoon) who convulsed himself and roared with laughter.

He put Tom Moore in hysterics, made him cry at breakfast and leave the table. Mrs. Siddons tried to resist him and keep her tragic dignity; she ended by flinging herself back in her chair in such a prolonged paroxysm that the company at dinner was alarmed (though Sydney Smith doubted she ever really departed from tragedy. She used to *stab* the potatoes).

At dinner parties the servants choked to hear him and ran from the room to hide their smiles. Sir James Mackintosh was reported red in the face rolling on the floor in fits of laughter. His sayings sent Queen Victoria into spasms when they were repeated to her—admittedly not a fair test of wit, Smith would agree. Even when he attempted to be serious, he was likely to be misunderstood. Once while he was saying grace before dinner, a young lady at the table laughed out loud: "Oh, Mr. Smith, you are always so amusing!"

He was so amusing that he was invited to meet himself. An absent-minded acquaintance, Lord Dudley, stopped him on the street and said, "Dine with me today, and I will get Sydney Smith to meet you." Smith confessed the temptation was great, but he had another engagement.

He easily forgave a piece of absent-mindedness as a man able to forget his own name:

"I knocked at a door in London; asked, 'Is Mr. B. at home?'

" 'Yes, sir, pray what name shall I say?'

"What name? what name? Ay, that is the question. What is my name? . . . At last, to my great relief, it flashed across me that I was Sydney Smith."

He told about a forgetful clergyman (himself?) who jogged along the road one day till he came to a turnpike.

"What is to pay?"

"Pay, sir, for what?"

"Why, for my horse, to be sure."

"Your horse, sir? What horse? There is no horse, sir."

"No horse? God bless me!" said the clergyman, looking down between his legs. "I thought I was on horseback."

He laughed and he chose to laugh. Sydney Smith believed in happiness as a necessary choice, the real object of existence, "the grammar of life," then lived as if happiness were his to command, escaping any tendency to self-pity. It was only common sense to be happy, to accept the obligation not to be unhappy.

"The world is full of all sorts of sorrows and miseries —and I think it is better never to have been born," he wrote Lady Holland on the death of her young daughter. "But when evils have happened turn away your mind from them as soon as you can to everything of good which remains. Most people grieve as if grief were a duty, or a pleasure, but all who can control it should control it."

He spoke in certain knowledge of what grief is, out of his own griefs. Two of his children died in infancy (he who adored children and wished he could afford to have twenty; who hoped his daughter Saba would be born with one eye so that he might never lose her). His son Wyndham grew up to misbehave so abominably his father refused to mention his name. In his will, Sydney Smith left him an allowance of £200 a year on condition that Wyndham keep away from his mother's house and leave her alone. The terrible tragedy in his life was the death at twenty-four of his other son, Douglas. If he never fully recovered from that loss, he let no one share his pain. The fits of black depression that attacked him Sydney Smith suffered in private; his low spirits he kept to himself. His jesting advice was: "Short views of human life—not further than dinner or tea."

Short views of life, that was it: words against woe. "Take short views—hope for the best—trust in God." Never give way to melancholy. Never listen to music in a minor key. Never extort friendship with a cocked pistol. Live as well as you dare. The question is, are you happy now? Are you likely to remain so till this evening?

No one could call Sydney Smith shy (Harriet Martineau, who was deaf, said he talked like the great bell of St. Paul's). Yet he had cured himself of shyness by two discoveries:

1. "That all mankind were not solely employed in observing me."

2. "That shamming was no use, that the world was very clearsighted and soon estimated a man at his just value."

A comfortable house was one source of happiness ("It ranks immediately after health and a good conscience"). A good digestion was part of the secret, since "character, talents, virtues, and qualities, are powerfully affected by beef, mutton, pie-crust, and rich soups." Indigestion caused most of the miseries of body and mind. A man might sink in despair after eating lobster. "In the same manner old friendships are destroyed by toasted cheese."

This is impressive comment from one known as a table wit, because he was funny at dinner, which fed his sense of humor. Yet he thrived on banter, not on monologue that he found uncivil and tedious. He loved to talk as well as eat and used to hold on to his plate to keep the servants from snatching it away.

"You must take a walk on an empty stomach," a doctor told him once when he was ill.

"Whose?" he inquired.

Having decided to abstain from strong drink, he listed for Lady Holland the advantages of doing so: "1st, sweet sleep; having never known what sleep was I sleep like a baby or a ploughboy. If I wake, no needless terror, no black views of life, but pleasing hope and pleasing recollection. . . . If I dream, it is not of lyons and tygers, but of Love—and Tithes. 2ndly I can take longer walks and make greater exertions without fatigue. My understanding is improved, and I comprehend Political Economy. . . . Only one evil ensues from it: I am in such extravagant spirits that I must lose blood, or look out for some one who will bore and depress me. Pray leave off wine."

As for old age when he reached it, Sydney Smith found the last years not unlike the rest, on the whole agreeable. "I am quite well, enjoying life, and ready for death," he wrote his friend Lady Grey. He continued to be amusing and amused, much given to talking, laughing, and noise. He refused to live with death in his heart.

"It is a bore, I admit, to be past seventy," but at seventy-three: "My animal spirits do not desert me." At seventy-four: "I can neither walk nor breathe, but in other particulars am well."

Shortly before he died in that year, Sydney Smith made a final report, or perhaps it was a testimonial: "I am, upon the whole, a happy man, have found the world an entertaining place, and am thankful to providence for the part allotted to me in it."

A gracious word of thanks from a fast forgiver.

He had called Daniel Webster a steam engine in trousers, Macauley a book in breeches. Sydney Smith was a nice person in a cassock.

'Tis Good Sleeping in a Whole Skin

(The title of a lost Elizabethan play)

Sometimes I'm ashamed of the types
I take to bed—
The weirdos, the fags, the dirty old men
(Just what I need)—
Remembering that the Rev. Sydney Smith once said,
"Live always in the best company
When you read."
So I will live with the Metaphysical Poets,
And I will sleep with Sydney Smith abed,
Composed and comforted.

Beautiful Lofty Astronauts

On February 20, 1962, in my class in modern poetry that begins at 9:20 A.M., two students brought along their transistor radios. Though from time to time I had ruled out knitting, gum chewing, cola drinking, daydreaming, and other diversions, I hadn't thought to object to radio listening before. John Glenn was about to be launched into what we used to call the sky, now outer space—the first human American in orbit (they had sent up a chimpanzee named Enos the previous November, besides three black mice who took a free trip back in October, 1960). And in fact he did set off halfway through the class period, at 9:48 according to transistor radio.

For once I was ready to abandon poetry, unwilling to offer up Dylan Thomas as a counter attraction. Then I pulled myself together. "Let's get to work," I said. "Either John Glenn will improve the flight of Dylan Thomas or the other way round. We can't lose."

My radio listeners kept one ear tuned to the space man, the other to the poet. We went on reading Thomas, a high soarer himself:

> Not for the proud man apart
> From the raging moon I write
> On these spindrift pages . . .

By the end of the hour, Colonel Glenn was in orbit over Africa, at 17,000 miles an hour. He kept going all morning, and so did I. He circled the planet three times, saw three sunrises and sunsets, and traced the outline of the state of Florida. Luminous particles like fireflies hung suspended beyond his window.

On his way back to "this pendent world, in bigness as a star," riding in a silver spacesuit inside a 10-foot capsule called the *Friendship 7*, John Glenn passed through temperatures of 4,000 degrees Fahrenheit that might have shriveled him into flame.

Moved to poetry himself, he remarked aloud, "Boy, that was a real fireball!"

Five years before, in 1957, while visiting a state fair, E. B. White (a poet) looked appreciatively about him and said, "I see nothing in space as promising as the view from a ferris wheel."

He may be right. Yet it seems to me a poet belongs a little higher up than that, the more weightless and disembodied the better. With his head already in the clouds, a watcher of the skies, a confirmed traveler to Venus, he has long made these lunar flights into the unknown, thriving on moonmist. Lunacy is a poet's heritage.

So if they are still planning future trips to the moon, on to Venus and the outer stars, or if by now they're looking for infinity, they had better take a poet along. He might even settle for finity. Poets know a lot about finity.

But when will they send a *word* man up there? Major Gordon Cooper rocketed alone into empty space, following Scott Carpenter (3 orbits) and Walter Schirra (6 orbits), on a spectacular 22-orbit flight, May 15–16, 1963. Faced with the miracle of heaven and earth, he lapsed into rhapsody: "It feels good, buddy! It's great sport!"

On his heroic return from some 150 miles up, bringing down his ship the *Faith 7* neatly on target ("right on the old gazoo") in a harrowing splashdown through failure of the automatic controls, he looked staggered and told reporters: "I agree with the other fellows—*wow!*"

The words, dear Brutus, are not in the stars but in ourselves.

In July, 1966, with the astronauts by now blasting into orbit two men at a time, Mike Collins and John Young found themselves 476 miles up in the Gemini 10 flight. Collins took a space walk in a suit like a coat of armor, moving fearlessly in a stroll at 17,500 miles an hour (a celestial statistic). But he wasn't out there to describe the scenery, that

Illimitable ocean without bound,
Without dimension: where length, breadth, and height
And time, and place are lost . . .

"Everything outside is about like we predicted," he said, climbing back in. Collins and Young were called the most untalkative men who ever went into space. After the splashdown, they told a waiting world Columbus was right, the world is round. Like small boys, "We've had a lot of fun," they said, whatever Columbus may have murmured on arrival.

In October, 1968, the Apollo 7 spaceship, with three aboard, command pilot Walter Schirra, astronauts Donn Eisele and Walter Cunningham, made an eleven-day flight during which they pursued an orbiting Saturn rocket. Firing the ship's big rocket engine, Schirra exclaimed, "Yaba daba doo!", came within 70 feet of the tumbling rocket "right up the pike," and jammed on his brakes.

During the 163 times they circled this planet, Schirra complained he had a cold in the head and his windows were dirty. Once he gazed down into the furious whirling vortex of Hurricane Gladys. "Really a doozy," said Schirra.

On December 21, 1968, Apollo 8 took Frank Borman, James Lovell, William Anders, and the Hong Kong flu on a six-day flight to the moon and back. They accelerated to 24,000 miles an hour, faster than man had ever flown, left the earth's orbit, and on Christmas Eve were circling 70 miles above the moon to see what it looked like on her backside, which she hasn't yet turned toward the earth. (Henry Vaughan, poet: "How brave a prospect is a bright backside.") It looked, they said, like dirty beach sand with lots of footprints in it. They took turns reading aloud on a telecast the first ten verses of Genesis.

After splashdown, Borman was asked what the moon was made of, and without fear of contradiction he said, "It's not green cheese. It's made of American cheese."

Then, on Sunday, July 20, 1969, the mission was accomplished, we landed on the moon, moonwalkers; and the earth from there looked like a child's blue ball spinning in the sky. In the epic of Apollo 11, Neil Armstrong became the first man to touch the moon's surface, managing to say a few well-chosen immortal words: "That's one small step for a man, one giant leap for mankind." In the Sea of Tranquillity, too.

Buzz Aldrin followed close behind, down the nine rungs of the ladder. "Beautiful, beautiful, beautiful," he said. They stayed twenty-one hours. Like two weird moonmen, wearing lunar overshoes, they bounded gingerly among the dusty craters picking up pieces of the moon in a slow game of hopscotch (what else is there to do?), romping in kangaroo hops to bring back the moon's mysterious story, perhaps a clue to the birth of the solar system, the story of Creation.

It looked a poor sort of place, not silver at all, not love-lit (the poets have misled us), only a god-and-man-forsaken desert, a lot of nothingness. It never bore fifty daughters to Endymion.

Down here on earth, we had two planets in view, the moon and Chappaquiddick, like the title of a song (a dead moon and a dead girl), with closeups now and then of the war dead in Vietnam. Down here too a moonstruck poet wrote a poem, which was published in *Life* two weeks before the astronauts landed. In "Moon Ground," James Dickey tried to imagine himself on the moon, picking up his quota of rocks. But as he wandered bemused, the only words that came to his mind with a poetic ring to them were, comically enough, from Gray's "Elegy in a Country Churchyard":

> Now fades the glimmering landscape on the sight,
> And all the air a solemn stillness holds.

Even at that, in the weightlessness up there, Dickey was too dazed to remember the lines as iambic pentameter:

> My massive clothes bubble around me
> Crackling with static and Gray's
> Elegy helplessly coming
> From my heart, and I say I think something
> From high school I remember now
> Fades the glimmering landscape on the sight and all the air
> A solemn stillness holds.

Or he might have quoted a couplet from Pope:

> What would this man? Now upward will he soar,
> And little less than angel, would be more.

The Apollo Moon Missions continued thick and fast for the next three years. On the second moon landing, Charles

Conrad and Alan Bean of Apollo 12 parked in the Sea of Storms, sounding on arrival like a vaudeville team: "Whoopee, man! Holy cow! Son of a gun! Ho, ho, ho, hey!" Al Bean described the place as the color of concrete like his own driveway. Edgar Mitchell of Apollo 14 thought it resembled plaster of Paris. John Young of Apollo 16 said, "It looks like a marshmallow float."

W. H. Auden also wrote a poem, "Moon Landing." He called the enterprise "a phallic triumph,"

> an adventure
> it would not have occurred to women
> to think worth while.

But whom was he praising—women or astronauts?

Women like poets must be content to bear witness. I saw the launching of Apollo 15 from a friend's house on Merritt Island, Florida, beside the Banana River where the river-birds—pelicans and white herons—with vast unconcern searched for fish or flew low overhead. Straight across the horizon, six miles away, stood Apollo 15, 363 feet tall on Pad 39A, ready for takeoff. The sun shone, with little cloud. From inside the house we could hear the countdown on the television set.

More than a million watchers had gathered for miles around, many of them lined up across the river. Two hundred private planes were said to be in the sky, a thousand private boats in the nearby waters.

6-5-4-3-2-1. 9:34 A.M. exactly. With the tremendous firing at the base, spreading flames as if an atomic explosion were to follow, the rocket stood poised. On its red blazing tail it began to soar, streaking upward like a skyrocket that would burst into colored stars. Far, far off in the sky we saw the booster section drop and fall like a parachute into the ocean. And it was gone, on man's fourth trip to the moon.

At the spectacle I was more inarticulate than the astronauts, full of gasps and worn-out adjectives. *Fantastic,* I said, *simply fantastic! Well,* I said, *for Pete's sake—*

Finally, in December, 1972, the whole moon undertaking came to an abrupt end. Apollo 17, in a fiery departure the night of December 8, completed the last planned trip to the moon in the twentieth century. Gene Cernan and Jack Schmitt became the eleventh and twelfth men to step on the moon, taking with them for the farewell journey five desert mice but no women and no poets. A dozen men had visited another planet; then it was over. On earth we had too many unsolved problems to try it again.

Billed on television as "The Last Voyage to the Moon," which sounded like science fiction, Cernan and Schmitt (a professional scientist) landed in the valley of Taurus-Littrow.

"We is here, man, we is here," cried Cernan, and as they tumbled around in the slippery dust he sang. "Oh bury me not on the lone prairie."

They traveled in a $12.9-million moon car for twenty miles to explore mountains, valleys, gorges, craters, where temperatures ranged from 243° above zero in blinding sunlight to 257° below zero in moon darkness. They lost a fender on the moon car. They found some bright-orange soil, a new shade in moondust, and left for home with 334 pounds of rock and dirt. At last report, the moon and its birth remained pretty much of a mystery.

I don't know whether the five moonmice made it safely back or not.

The Armchair Astronomer

"Britain's new Astronomer Royal thinks all the
talk about interplanetary travel is 'utter bilge.' "
—News item, 1955

1955

The Astronomer Royal means to cope
With Heaven through a telescope,
Nor from his armchair stir at all
To regions astronomical:
He looks in scorn at the starry skies
As worlds to conquer or Anglicize,
Unlike Browning, who looked before
And murmured, "What's a Heaven for?"

1969

At least if Heaven there be—a place
In interplanetary space—
By God, we're nearer than we were,
Aren't we, Royal Astronomer?

The Felicity of Madame de Sévigné

Sainte-Beuve called her a laughing blonde. She was, he thought, charming, unaffectedly beautiful, a lady loved and lovable, a writer of light and graceful simplicity, "*écrivain adorable.*" Her cousin, Comte de Bussy, called her "*la plus aimable femme du monde*": "I do not believe there is a person in the world more generally beloved than yourself."

Yet there are those who find her frivolous by nature, a hypocrite, a poseur, a false and mindless creature. Sir Harold Nicolson denied her stature as a human being, intimating she was, after all, only a woman and a silly one at that.

She was animated, she appeared happy, a radiant person who loved laughter. Her closest friend, Madame de la Fayette, wrote to her, "Joy is the true element of your soul and unhappiness more alien to you than to any other person in the world." I wish it were so.

Madame de Sévigné became a widow at twenty-five, when her debauched and faithless husband was killed in a duel over a woman. His love affairs had been the talk of Paris, in particular the liaison with Ninon de L'Enclos, who became successively through the years the mistress of Madame de Sévigné's husband, of Madame de Sévigné's son, and, it seems, of Madame de Sévigné's grandson.

The portraits of the notorious Ninon show her long-nosed and vapid, though when she died at ninety she was credited with still possessing her abundant physical charms and given perhaps undue credit on her tombstone: "*Elle fut renommée pour sa chasteté pendant les dernières années de sa vie.*"

In the letters to her daughter, Madame de Sévigné shows

194

deep concern over her son's ridiculous pursuit of Ninon (who was fifty-one to his twenty-three). On March 13, 1671, she wrote: "Your brother wears the chains of Ninon. . . . she corrupted the morals of his father." On April 1 following: "Mme de la Fayette and I are doing all we can to remove him from this dangerous connection." On April 8: "Ninon has dismissed him. This was a great relief to me." On April 22: "Ninon has quite given him up. . . . She said the other day, 'His mind is like porridge, his body is like wet paper, and his heart is like a pumpkin fried in snow.' " Her son Charles, reflected his mother, had the soul of a lunatic with a mind like whipped cream.

Earlier in the year, February, 1671, at the age of forty-five, Madame de Sévigné suffered her first agonizing separation from her daughter, when Françoise became the Comtesse de Grignan and left Paris to join her husband in Provence. As the carriage rumbled off taking Françoise away, Madame thought of throwing herself from the window in grief. She sobbed for five hours without ceasing. "I cannot be happy without you," she wrote. "It is useless to pretend I can ever be happy for a moment without you." From that day her life was empty.

For the next twenty-five years, till she died, beginning a fresh letter as she finished one, she poured out her love to her *très-chère,* her divine one, "the only passion of my soul," the grief and joy of all her days. Her love was a preoccupation, an extravagance, an obsession. And the knowledge that her cold, proud daughter didn't return that love was an unbearable and incurable hurt.

"Love me," she pleaded. "I embrace you body and soul." "I truly believe nothing can equal the depth of my passion for you." "I love you so passionately that I hide a great part of my love not to oppress you with it." "You are the main purpose of my existence." "My heart is filled with your image, beautiful one, to the exclusion of all else." "I exist for you alone, would that God's grace might one day inspire me to love Him as I do you." "I thirst for you as we should for our salvation." "Were I to attempt to make you understand all the bitterness and pain . . ."

Madame de Grignan wrote her mother dutifully twice a week. But since after her death her own daughter, Pauline, destroyed all these letters (before preparing for publication those of her grandmother, Madame de Sévigné), one can only guess at the frictions, the resentments expressed, the rebukes, the cruel indifference. In June, 1677, for example, Françoise to her mother's despair had made the "abominable suggestion and made with unctuous satisfaction that you and I would be better apart."

"*Je suis une pleureuse*," wrote Madame. "Ofttimes when I weep I dare not tell you lest I draw down on my head your well-deserved reproaches." She slept badly. She had frequent depressions and forebodings. When the post was late she was frantic. Virginia Woolf says in an essay about her, "It was a passion that was twisted and morbid; it caused her many humiliations; sometimes it made her ashamed of herself."

The mistake, of course, of an otherwise reasonable woman was to love anyone to distraction, with such unwanted solicitude, such outpourings, as she said, "far surpassing what is common to mankind." Sometimes her aching words seem to fall into poetry:

> Every place reminds me of you,
> and a sword has entered my soul.
>
> I search everywhere in vain
> for my dear child,
> and I find her not.

> I have seen Madame d'Amelot too,
> she weeps well.
> I am an excellent judge of weeping.
>
> *Je laisse tout*
> *dans les mains de Dieu.*

Three months before her death she wrote, *"J'ai fait mon rôle."* I wonder what she thought it was. She was a lady felicitous and full of grace, lovable and loving. But did she call herself happy? I wonder.

The Lady of the Château

*"Je me ménage les délices
d'un adieu charmant."*
        —From a letter to her daughter

I would be wise like Madame de Sévigné,
Had I too her *sagesse*. Yet to be wise
Is to possess a like felicity,
So amiable she stands before my eyes,
The lady of the château. In sunlight,
She lingers in her doorway (she who loved
The wisdom of a hospitable house,
The testimony of the bread and wine)
And listens smiling to the gritty sound
Of fast-departing coach wheels. She reflects,
As (*toujours sage*) one takes a tolerant view,
That tiresome guests are often pleasantest—
So perfect is dull company homebound,
So heart-consoling is the last adieu.

Wife to Simon Bradstreet

Simon her husband brought her to Massachusetts when she was a young and happy eighteen, to exile in the new country. For more than forty years her frontier life on a farm near the Merrimac River was beset with hardship and disaster so constant that she worried about her straying soul, too much in love with the world, and God's chastisement. "I saw the Lord sent to humble and try me and doe mee good," because the Lord knew she needed correction, being too wayward like "an untoward child." She died three hundred years ago, and nobody knows where she was buried or even what she looked like.

Yet Anne Bradstreet was a comely wife, I'm sure, and a poet. A little of her poetry lives and speaks for her—not in the stilted literary verse or heavy meditations, not in her depressing works on the four elements, the four humors, the four ages of man, the four seasons, and the four monarchies (how did she happen to overlook the Four Quartets?). They were arid and ponderous, but she was not. She thought so ill of her first book with its grandiose title (*The Tenth Muse Lately Sprung Up in America*, published in England by her brother-in-law without her consent) that she called it her "rambling brat" and blushed to own it, casting it from her as unfit for light, the "ill-form'd offspring of my feeble brain."

She was in fact a passionate Puritan, a woman who regretted the way we shorten our short days, "Living so little while we are alive," a woman deeply in love, supremely happy in marriage, who gladly followed Simon, dear and loving husband, to the ends of the earth. ("I prize thy love more than whole mines of gold.")

199

Simon, she told him in urgent letters, was her head, heart, eyes, life, joy, and more, her "magazine of earthly store." She bewailed their separation even for a night: "How stayest thou there, whilst I at Ipswich lie?" "Return," she cried, "my dear, my joy, my only love."

> If ever two were one, then surely we,
> If ever man were loved by wife, then thee,
> If ever wife was happy in a man,
> Compare with me ye women if you can.

It was the love affair with Simon that made her a poet. And, though it pleased God to keep her a long time without a child, she was lucky in love, blessed eight times over:

> I had eight birds hatched in one nest;
> Four cocks there were, and hens the rest:
> I nursed them up with pains and care,
> For cost nor labor did I spare;
> Till at last they felt their wing,
> Mounted the trees and learned to sing.

Words for Anne Bradstreet

Say it is love. Say not untruly
That by God's ordinance, Simon, it is so.
Or if it wants twice saying, come to me,
And by my knowing what (thou knowest) I know
I will advise thee of a certainty
'Tis so, Simon. 'Tis so because 'tis so.

Dylan Thomas, Hellgazer and Rejoicer

Sir John Mandeville, the great traveler, who was somewhat given to lying, honestly admitted he did not visit the Garden of Eden. "Of Paradys ne can I speken properly, for I was not there."

I talk a lot in the classroom about hell, into which the hellgazers insist on gazing and occasionally falling. I am by now something of an authority on hell—its look, its nature, its dreary inhabitants. I only wish writers could agree as to where and what hell is. Instead they contradict each other flatly, today more than ever, while you and I go on peering into a dungeon of everlasting hellfire below our feet as heaven is above our eyes. Yet in the *Odyssey* it is on the earth's verge. In *Paradise Lost* it is a separate kingdom carved out of chaos. In the *Divine Comedy* it is right with us on this planet, a huge pit formed in concentric circles for the abode of the ungodly.

There are so many hells and hellgazers. Whatever the location or address, it speaks man's sense of guilt and punishment, his despairing need to feast on suffering, perdition, eternal misery and woe. James Joyce, in *A Portrait of the Artist As a Young Man*, gazed into the ultimate physical hell, full of fiends, as it was presented to the Dublin schoolboys of Belvedere School by the Jesuit priests. Hell is a deep foul-smelling prison with walls four thousand miles thick, filled with the stench of a vast choking sewer, where a consuming fire of unspeakable fury attacks the sinners till the blood seethes in the veins, the brain boils, the heart glows and bursts, the bowels turn to a red-hot bubbling mass, the eyes are flaming melted balls. "HELL! HELL! HELL! HELL!" cries Stephen Dedalus, frightened out of his senses by the picture of his own damnation given him by his kindly teachers.

Yet Shaw, in *Man and Superman*, recommended hell as a livelier more congenial spot than heaven throughout eternity. The best people prefer to go there, since the Devil has fairly won in the struggle with God. Hell is the true paradise of men, a wicked domain but relaxed and easygoing, far pleasanter than the real hell man has created on earth.

This hell on earth is what worries me—not in the next world (as it used to be situated) but exclusively in this one, viable and real, invading the home. Archibald MacLeish, in *J.B.*, the modern drama of Job, shows hell to be existence itself, merely to be alive, to see, to feel, to suffer. In Sartre's *No Exit*, hell is other people. Hell is being locked in a bleak hotel room with a couple of other sinners, never to escape their appalling hate, never to be alone. Never.

The poets are accomplished hellgazers, professional in their view as extinguishers of hope, some of them wallowing in the terrors of this planet. A century ago Baudelaire found hell on the streets of Paris with its depravity and evil, its putrid corpses and reeking sewers. In *"Une Charogne,"* he took his girl to see a decomposing female corpse in a lewd position, being eaten by maggots. "And you too shall be like this filthy excrement," he told her, "This horrible infection, / Star of my eyes." (But I like better the little song *"La Charogne"* I used to sing as a child:

> *Tout le monde pue*
> *Comme la charogne*
> *Sauve que le petit Jésus*
> *Qui sent d'eau de cologne.*)

Rimbaud wrote with simple charm in *Une Saison en Enfer*: "I believe myself in hell; hence I am there."

For years T. S. Eliot was fanned by the flames of hell-fire till he drew back in recoil from the edge of the pit and followed after Dante in the purgatorial climb toward the summit of the mountain. Unlike Sartre, Eliot declared that hell is being alone. Hell is oneself—unloved, incapable of loving, lost in a prison of self where other people are merely projections: "One is always alone."

No, worse than that, said W. H. Auden, gazing into a dark corner of it. ("Hell is hard to bear" says his poem entitled "Hell.") Hell is the psychiatrist's couch, the hangman's shed for us lonelies, who live our horrified lives in a perpetual nightmare of self-loathing, angst, hate, negation, "terror and concupiscence and pride." For hellgazers, the mind is its own hell—any answer will do. Hell is existence. Hell is other people. Hell is loneliness. "I myself am hell," said Robert Lowell. Hell is myself.

On the other hand heaven, so the rejoicers say, is also myself. Heaven is being alive. The ability to say yes outweighs the rejection of life, faith is stronger than despair. In our age of peril and intermittent threat of extinction, the sun still shines, lovers still kiss, *die Welt ist schön, die Himmel ist blau*. The choice, they say, is still in favor of living with some kind of joy.

But the rejoicers, the advocates, contradict themselves as often as the hellgazers. Though sanguine, they never for a moment agree on what to rejoice about. You would think offhand they would simply seek pleasure over pain, as Eliot finally did when he got his vision back, taking the long dark way from hell to heaven on a journey of humility and penitence.

"Consequently I rejoice," he said, "having to construct something / Upon which to rejoice."

Yet the quest was hardly a merry one. You don't hear him whistling or laughing along the weary road to Little Gidding.

Wallace Stevens was aware of taking his own direction: "Eliot and I are dead opposites and I have been doing about everything that he would not be likely to do." In "Sunday Morning," Stevens wrote a poem of this earth, a place of rejoicing where we live on an island in the endless water, free of either heaven or hell, unsponsored by any God. As an unbeliever, he believed in heaven on earth, the only heaven we shall know, strictly contradicting Eliot's defeated view of the world as a wasteland. To Stevens this was no desert where we die of spiritual thirst but a green, fertile garden, a paradise found. We are, he said, "An unhappy people in a happy world." Accept it, the beauty of the reality. Accept the garden.

Hopkins had rejoiced by saying yes to God ("I did say yes O at lightning and lashed rod"). And in his opposite, contrary way E. E. Cummings took up the refrain. "We'll make yes," he said, "the world is yes through love," "love is the every only god." Early in life he constructed his own pagan world of yes and occupied it in a carnival of rejoicing, "to heaven with hell" as his motto.

What was Dylan Thomas then, hellgazer or rejoicer? He was both, I think, depending on what time of day he asked himself, in what moment of hell or heaven. He was a rejoicer who told John Malcolm Brinnin he had seen more than once the Gates of Hell. In "The Doctor and the Devils," he wrote, "Lord, but it's a happy time . . . even in the unhappy time."

While endorsing life, he admitted his terror of it. Fearful of mortality, he clung to his brief sojourn, to the griefs of being, with a sense of splendor and heartache. Yeats had said it before, calling it tragic joy—we begin to live joyously only when we conceive of life as a tragedy. Dylan Thomas lived and wrote in tragic and tempestuous joy, advancing with fury through his numbered days to the barking of the hellhounds. "Tell him [a critic]," he wrote Pamela Johnson in 1934, "I write of worms and corruption, because I *like* worms and corruption."

In *Under Milk Wood* he gave his version of life to both the pious and the bawdy: to old Mary Ann Sailors, who believed the town was the Chosen Land ("She is not at all mad; she merely believes in Heaven on earth"), and to the town prostitute, Polly Garter, who loved them all, Tom, Dick, and Harry, but most of all she loved life. Life is a terrible thing, she said, thank God for that.

Contradictory was the word for Dylan—a Welshman who couldn't speak Welsh; a man who loved the sea and couldn't swim; a poet who watched the herons along the shore and saw them walking now like priests and hymning saints, now like women poets. In person he looked contradictory, small and fat, grubby and rumpled, hardly the portrait of a young faun Augustus John made of him, hardly the figure of a bard.

When I met him six months before his death, on the night of May 12, 1953, I thought him the limit, a beer drinking, potbelly, snub-nosed, comical devil, yet with a sweetness and modesty about him that denied his tendency to strut. His curly hair was wet with sweat to find himself cornered by academics. His thick lips trembled. One could imagine him through embarrassment bursting into tears or obscenities. Though he read his poems those days at the universities, one could see he disliked the halls of learning, quick to proclaim himself an ignoramus who had never gone to college, had read no books (a great lie, of course).

If asked about other contemporary poets, he shrugged. "I don't know any." He wasn't clever at small talk or witty. He ventured no opinions. He said he hated reading his poems aloud.

Yet there were the extraordinary words in his head. When he spoke them to an audience, his voice was exalted, the most strangely heroic voice I've ever heard. He began with his vulgar prose piece, "A Visit to America," shifted to a finer note with Yeats's "Lapis Lazuli" and "John Kinsella's Lament for Mrs. Mary Moore,"

> What shall I do for pretty girls
> Now my old bawd is dead?

and continued sublime with his own rhapsodic "Fern Hill" and

> Do not go gentle into that good night.
> Rage, rage against the dying of the light.

In spite of the ill fame that had preceded him (how he appeared on the lecture platform sodden with drink and disorderly, how he belched in people's faces, pursued scandalized lady professors and complimented them on their golden breasts), he wasn't outrageous in the least. He was sad and splendid. With all the chain smoking and compulsive beer drinking that night, the sense he gave of being self-destructive and somehow doomed, I kept thinking of having read he would rewrite a line of verse fifty or a hundred times—a craftsman who knew "the peace that is a poem." You wouldn't believe it to look at him.

"A poet is a poet for such a very tiny bit of his life; for the rest, he is a human being."

—Dylan Thomas

Under the Milkwood Tree

(Song for Male Voices in *Under Milk Wood*)

Under the milkwood tree,
Who loves to lie with me?
"Oh, isn't life a terrible thing,
Thank God!" says Mistress Polly.

"Oh, isn't life," rejoices she,
"Terrible under the milkwood tree!"
Polly, I know, would be the first
To say, thank God, this is the worst.

"Oh, Tom and Dick and Harry, folly
Is all life is," she cries, "but jolly!"
Then whither shall I follow Polly?
To the milkwood, milkwood tree.

A Nun, a Girl, and Gerard Manley Hopkins

In my poetry class we were reading Hopkins's "The Wreck of the Deutschland," that stupendous drama of shipwreck —the true and tragic tale of a ship called the *Deutschland* that, between midnight and morning of December 7, 1875, on her way from Bremen to America, foundered on a sand bar at the mouth of the Thames. In the dark, during a blizzard of wind and snow, she struck a smother of sand and was wrecked there. Of the 213 aboard her, seventy-eight lives were lost, their bodies crushed and drowned, washed into the snow-driven sea. Sailors climbed into the rigging to save themselves, while women and children screamed in terror below. One seaman out of pity tied a rope around his waist and descended, only to be dashed against the side of the ship and decapitated. There he dangled like a pendulum, the headless corpse, to and fro in the roaring storm. Among the women, five Franciscan nuns, exiled from Germany by the anti-Catholic Falk Laws, joined hands and died together. The Rhine had rejected them, the Thames killed them. "Five! the finding and sake / And cipher of suffering Christ."

It was the death of one of the five—the Nun, the chief sister—that Hopkins sought to understand. She rose a lioness towering in the tumult above the women wailing and the children bawling, and as the night howled and the sea romped over the deck to drown them cried out before she perished, "O Christ, Christ, come quickly."

"The majesty! What did she mean?" Hopkins asks the question in wonder and grief. At the moment of death, why did she make her majestic cry? Or, rather, he asks, what did she *not* mean? With mounting tension he considers one by one all the things she could not have meant:

She did not merely seek to die, calling to Death as a lover to free her from the horror and anguish of this night. She did not cry out for the crown then, for the martyrdom that Christ had suffered before her. She was not begging with these words for the lovely treasure of heaven. She was not seeking for herself either safety or reward. She was not asking ease for her "sodden-with-its-sorrowing heart." She called to him not out of fear, or, blinded by the "sloggering brine," out of the appeal of Christ's own Passion, to relive his own death. No. It was not any of these.

It was something else, something the Nun saw. Choking, gasping for breath, seeking to comprehend, Hopkins reaches at last the question: what *did* she mean? What must she have meant? Struggling to speak, he seems to be drowning like her. He labors to say it, pants to make it plain, find the simple words for it.

Do you see? he cries. "Strike you the sight of it? look at it loom there"—and there it is. Hopkins knows. He knows! The vision of the Master has transfigured her. Christ has appeared to her, he has come, he is there—Himself, *ipse*, to save the Nun, to cure her of death. He is walking on the waves toward her. He has arrived in the storm to save her and take her home,

the Master,
Ipse, the only one, Christ, King, Head:
He was to cure the extremity where he had cast her.

As I read aloud these words of the poem, in a sudden burst a girl in the class broke into uncontrolled weeping. With streaming face, she wept. For the last seven stanzas, during which Hopkins adores the wisdom and mastery of God, she wept, her wailing voice rising higher than the Nun's cry, while the students on either side of her turned to embrace and wipe away her tears and comfort her.

The rest of the class sat stunned. The room grew electric, charged with their silence. If any had been quietly dozing or daydreaming, they were shocked into attention, staring with blank astonishment first at the weeping girl, then down at the open book in front of them. What impassioned message was this? What words were these? Only Hopkins's words? Hurled off one's feet by *Hopkins?*

As a performance, it seemed a bit theatrical. But, on the whole, I was more glad than sorry for it. A poem had spoken and been listened to. Only a few of them, perhaps, would remember the sound of the poetry or the story it told. One girl in particular will never forget. I think often of her face.

The Hoarder

"This to hoard unheard,
Heard unheeded, leaves me a lonely began."
—GERARD MANLEY HOPKINS

A beginner, unable to end
The beginning, is a lonely began,
Hoarder of words unheard,
Unheeded, novice and learner,
Still at the outset, still a beholder

Of golden coin in his keeping,
The heavenhoard, earthlovely treasure—
A hidden-of-heart beginner
Of words, still at the beginning,
Still at death still a lonely began.

The Wit of Wallace Stevens

I especially like his poem "The Man on the Dump" because it explains what a man does when he sits on a dump.
The dump is full of images—garbage and junk, a dead cat
in a paper bag, a wrapper from a can of pears, an old
corset, the janitor's poems, mattresses, bottles, muck and
dung. Or, if you see it that way, the dump is a garden of
flowers (azaleas and so on), where you enjoy yourself and
reject the trash.

"Ho-ho," laughs Stevens, what a nice place it is in spring,
at dawn, sunset, moonrise—a nice place the dump. When
the moon comes up to bassoon music above the old gray
elephant-colored automobile tires, "one sits and beats an
old tin can, lard pail" and one looks about and asks,

> Is it peace
> Is it a philosopher's honeymoon, one finds
> On the dump?

Is it here one finds the thing itself, the *the?* It has to be,
here if anywhere, since the world is a dump. In fact, it's
the only place left to look. Sitting on the dump, one makes a
choice of reality, whatever one wants to find and believe.
A sensible person or poet would hardly choose the garbage.

A man sits on a dump. A man also, being a man, makes
love as best he is able. Stevens wrote of middle-aged love
in "Le Monocle de Mon Oncle," about two lovers, their
bloom gone, splashed with frost, hanging "like warty
squashes, streaked and rayed."

> The laughing sky will see the two of us
> Washed into rinds by rotting winter rains.

The time is autumnal, and so are they; she is no longer "The radiant bubble that she was." What is this need to celebrate love at forty, singing wild anthems? Stevens trains his monocle on himself and smiles at the predicament. When amorists grow bald, how without absurdity do they give the virtuoso performance worthy of this great hymn? What bravura can he manage now? "I am a yeoman, as such fellows go."

Yet, he reflects, I made a lordly study of love in my youth and have some notion even now what it is about (Montaigne: "I knew them both; I have a right to speak"). Though properly I should be bidding love an appropriate mournful farewell, I seem to pursue it instead, stirred to greet the spring ("Shall I uncrumple this much-crumpled thing?"). Only last night, there was the pink magic—the spring lilacs, the chromatic stars. And there we were, you and I, two old timers, and the booming bullfrog—

> Last night, we sat beside a pool of pink
> Clippered with lilacs, scudding the bright chromes,
> Keen to the point of starlight, while a frog
> Boomed from his very belly, odious chords.

It is the bullfrog that upsets my students, who hear it as threat and prophecy, croaking on a late, bitter note. What kind of lovesong tuned to odious chords is this? But it doesn't worry me. I have heard the frogs at midnight, Master Shallow.

The truth is, says Stevens, "I pursued / And still pursue, the origin and course / Of love." Till reaching the declining age of forty I never knew what I know now: "I never knew / That fluttering things have so distinct a shade."

For St. Ursula, there was the love of the Lord. To my students, this poem of Stevens is at first meaningless. They don't understand a word of it, starting with the title in medieval French: "Cy Est Pourtraicte, Madame Ste Ursule, et les Unze Mille Vierges." By the time they figure out, or are told, that it says this is a portrait of St. Ursula and the 11,000 virgins, the poem begins to sound promising, full of multiplicity and abundance. Eleven *thousand* virgins?

Not many these days have heard of the wonderful legend of St. Ursula, who was a king's daughter in Brittany in the fourth century, a virgin of great beauty and a great love of the Lord. Gathering 11,000 maidens to her as companions, each as young, beautiful, and virginal as herself, she sailed off with them in eleven ships. When they disembarked at Cologne, after a trip on the Rhine, they were set upon by a hoard of Huns and all massacred, *die heilige Ursula und die elftausend Jungfrauen*. Ursula became a martyr and a saint defending her virginity, which she was determined to bestow on nobody but God.

In spite of the title, Stevens omits from the thirty-one short lines of the poem any mention whatever of the 11,000 virgins (presumably he lacked enough room), much to the disappointment of my students, who, still mystified, consider it a fraud.

The portrait he presents, not to be found in any book, is of Madame St. Ursula alone in a spring garden beside a bed of radishes. She is dressed not in a saint's habit but as a lady of medieval romance in red-and-gold brocade, looking as tempting as the red radishes she kneels upon the ground to gather. Just then the Lord enters his garden (whom she addresses fondly as "My dear"), and there on her knees where none can see—not before his altars but here in the green grass—she makes him a love offering of radishes and flowers,

> And then she wept
> For fear the Lord would not accept.

But the good Lord is pleased, if somewhat taken by surprise. He feels a strange and unexpected emotion, a throb, a stirring within him, "a subtle quiver, / That was not heavenly love. / Or pity." He feels not holy charity but human rapture. Madame St. Ursula is a beautiful lady virgin, the radishes are red and ravishing. And there you are.

"As a rule, people very much prefer to take the solemn views of poetry."

> —Wallace Stevens in a letter,
> November 25, 1935

I Sit Here Reading a Poet

(From Rilke, *The Notebooks of Malte Laurids Brigge*)

I sit here reading a poet,
And the poet tells me lightly
Read all the rest but come
To me for clarification.

The ultimate word on the subject
Issues from me, a poet.
The word is Love, of which I
Am the final authority.

So I read the poet, who knows
No more than I of the matter
But shares my absurd unknowing
And weeps my need to me.

D. H. Lawrence on Sex

D. H. Lawrence was a queer fellow to be an authority on sex. Yet it was as the utmost male he offered himself ("My sex is me"), one who must always serve, he said, in the real experience. "If I take my whole passionate, spiritual and physical love to the woman who in turn loves me, that is how I serve God."

He made a few confessions that sound inhibited coming from an expert. In a letter to Blanche Jennings, September 1, 1908, he wrote: "As for kissing—I never kiss but out of devilry—I hate slobber of all sorts." This from the kissing poet!

> I leaned me forward to find her lips,
> And claim her utterly in a kiss.

In a letter to Frieda, May 6, 1912, when he was taking her away from her husband and three children, he wrote: "I love you—but I always have to bite my tongue before I can say it. It's only my Englishness." On May 14 he was writing: "In our marriage, let us be businesslike. The love is there—then let the common-sense match it."

He asked Edward Garnett, "Why is it women *will* fall in love with me?"

> I wish I knew a woman
> who was like a red fire on the hearth
> glowing after the day's restless draughts ...
>
> and really take delight in her
> without having to make the polite effort of loving her.

"Surely," he wrote Willard Johnson in 1922, "I am man

enough to be able to think of my own organs with calm, even with indifference."

Lawrence angrily denied that *Lady Chatterley's Lover* was a sexual novel. It was phallic, like the gamekeeper Mellors. It had a phallic reality, a phallic awareness, a phallic insouciance. It was "the full fine flower with pistil and stamens standing"—far too tender a thing for a gross public to understand. It was "beautiful and tender and frail as the naked self, and I shrink very much even from having it typed."

He grew sick of people who considered him "a lurid sexuality specialist," preoccupied and obsessed, when all the while the sex relation was one he labored to make valid and respectable. ("About Lady C.—you mustn't think I advocate perpetual sex.") His religion, as he so often stated, was a belief in the blood, the flesh, as being wiser than the intellect. ("To know the *mind* of a woman is to end by hating her.") Out of the depth of the religious experience came the mystery of sexual fulfillment, which is Nature's holy plan. "Sex is the great uniter," said D. H. Lawrence.

It should be as natural as the goings on in "Love on the Farm," where

> The woodbine creeps abroad
> Calling low to her lover.

It should be as natural as his feeling for Black-Eyed Susan, his cow. There was a (platonic) relation between them: "And this relation is part of the mystery of love. . . . The queer cowy mystery of her is her changeless cowy desirableness."

> You tell me I am wrong,
> Who are you, who is anybody to tell me I am wrong?
> I am not wrong.

E. E. Cummings on Love

The word is love. When I was very young, I used to collect
definitions of love and keep them like limp spring violets
pressed in a book. For the most part they were wilted little
mementos, given to woe and complaint:

"Love's but a frailty of the mind" (Congreve). "Love
is a sickness full of woes" (Samuel Daniel). "Love is a
malady without a cure" (Dryden). "Oh, what a plague is
love! Oh, what a hell is this!" (Anon).

Chaucer thought well of it: "Love is a thing as any spirit
free." Robert Greene praised it lightly: "Ah, what is love!
It is a pretty thing."

Among modern poets it seems either missing from their
experience, or in serious trouble: "Love is a burnt match
skating in a urinal" (Hart Crane). "Love is the bone and
sinew of my curse" (Sylvia Plath). "Love's very fleas
are mine" (William Carlos Williams), as if love were a
mangy dog. Except, of course, for Cummings, the great
endorser and practitioner of love. He knew not only what
love is but where to find the girl, a celebrant, a yea sayer who
all his life never said no:

"Love is the every only god." "Love is more thicker
than forget." "Love is the sky and I am for you." "Love is
the whole and more than all."

Love escapes the machinemade unworld of mostpeople,
of the ungladly, the unlovers for whom unlove is unbeing,
who live wrongsideout and lonely in their unmysteries,
missing the formula for living which is wonderful 1 x 1.

For love are in you am in i are in we

Love is "my body when it is with your body," and a man who cannot love is not a man. Love is the "immeasurable is" of living. Love is the mating season, when it's spring and in spring anything can happen. Absolutely anything.

> wholly to be a fool
> while Spring is in the world
>
> my blood approves

When I met Mr. Cummings at a party one night after a poetry reading he had given at Duke University, we talked about love. Professionally, so to speak. It was very entertaining, and we appeared to agree perfectly. We believed in love at first sight, at second sight, at a glance, and at long last. He was a charmer, an easy man, attentive, bald with high cheekbones and with an old-fashioned courtesy (bowing over one's hand, smiling at every inanity one said) that made him seem gratified to find somebody to discuss love with.

As I say, we were in favor of it. He told me, after a while, that he had read a verse of mine in the *Atlantic Monthly*, inspired by a love poem of his own, or at least by the opening lines:

> be of love(a little)
> More careful
> Than of everything.

I was embarrassed. Having been caught out and faced with the liberty taken, I looked into his eyes to see if he was angry. He wasn't. He had exquisite manners, with all his capital letters and parentheses under control. I began to apologize for swiping his words.

Cummings laughed. "I liked it, and the honor is mine," he said. "What else is there to write about but love?"

"Nothing," I replied, "except death. You said it yourself, Mr. Cummings, 'alive is singing of love (what else is there to sing of?)' "

He took my hand, bent over and kissed it with grave decorum. "Look me up the next time you're in New York," he said.

Advice (a Little) Useful

"be of love(a little)
  More careful
  Than of everything."
      —E. E. CUMMINGS

Be of love (a little)
Artful,
Of the heaving breast, the cartful
Of endorsing sighs, the heart full,

Provident (a little)
Spareful
Of the puffery yet careful
Not to be of love too careful,

Not too coy (a little)
Lustful
And more trustful than distrustful—
As the brimming cup is just full,

Be of love oh more
Than needful
Amorous, my love, and deedful
But, as we were saying (heedful).

Beautiful Lofty Philosophers

Touchstone: "Hast any philosophy in thee, shepherd?"

Buddha was a great sitter. In his first trance, he sat apart under the cool shade of a rose-apple tree. For years (says Camus in *The Myth of Sisyphus*) he squatted motionless in the desert with his eyes on heaven, and the gods envied him his stony wisdom and the swallows built a nest in his outstretched hands. When the birds flew away, Buddha wept.

He went to sit under a Bo tree, where enlightenment occurred and the mynah birds, no doubt, perched on his head waiting for him to speak. After that, Buddha assumed the title of "The One Who Knows."

He meditated and said: "There is no companionship with a fool." "The world is enveloped in ignorance." "Cultivate equanimity."

A contemporary of Confucius wrote that in the good old days a naked virgin could travel the length of the kingdom of China carrying a bag of gold and she would not be molested. Neither flesh nor fleshpots tempted a man to lust. But since the plan was abandoned long ago, I presume it failed as a practical way to transport gold.

As for Confucius himself, he was a Man of Virtue 2,500 years ago, whose mother gave birth to him in a hollow mulberry tree. Confucius say: "I have never yet seen a man whose love of virtue equalled his love of woman."

Diogenes became a philosopher by the example set by a mouse. He saw a mouse whiffling about and admired its aimlessness. It was going and arriving nowhere. Having nowhere to get to, it reached no conclusions. But it was not afraid of the dark.

Montaigne admired Diogenes who, when called ignorant, a meddler with philosophy, agreed, saying, "I meddle with it all the more appropriately." He lived in the open air on dried figs and water and poured scorn on others for not doing likewise.

In Athens Plato defined a man: a two-legged animal without feathers. He was applauded. Diogenes plucked a cock, brought it to the Academy, and said, "This is Plato's man." Thereafter, four words had to be added to the definition of a man: "with broad flat nails."

Plato called him a dog. "Quite true," said Diogenes. "I fawn on those who give. I yelp at those who refuse. I bite rogues." Like a dog he ate, slept, and relieved himself in the marketplace without shame. When Alexander went to see Diogenes at Corinth, he introduced himself, "I am Alexander, surnamed the Great." Diogenes replied, "I am Diogenes, surnamed the Dog." And Plato said, "How much pride you show, Diogenes, by seeming not to be proud."

This is a world of fools, observed Diogenes. But he also said, "I am a citizen of the world." Philosopher to the end, he died in old age by simply holding his breath. The Corinthians erected a pillar to honor him, surmounting it with the figure of a dog and the words: "Say, dog, what do you guard in that tomb?"

"A dog."

"His name?"

"Diogenes."

Crates, a disciple of Diogenes and his most famous pupil, came from Thebes. Alexander may have lodged at Corinth in his house. When Alexander asked if he would like Thebes rebuilt, he said, "Why should it be? Another Alexander will destroy it again."

Crates was pursued by Hipparchia, who fell violently in love with him and threatened to kill herself unless she be allowed to marry him. Her wealthy parents implored Crates, who was penniless and ugly, to discourage her and change her mind. Like Diogenes, he sought virtue in having nothing. Deformed in body, he made himself hideous by wearing sheepskins in summer and a few rags in winter, stinking in the heat and freezing in the cold.

Unable to reason with Hipparchia, Crates stood up and took off his clothes, saying, "This is the bridegroom, here are his possessions. Now make your choice."

She chose him without hesitation and they were married, after which Hipparchia was called the female philosopher. She adopted his dress, and together they enjoyed a vagrant life, since long ago Crates had rejected his considerable wealth when Diogenes advised him to throw his money into the sea. With nowhere to lay their heads, they made passionate love in public.

"Hunger stops love, or, if not hunger, Time," remarked Crates, but lightly since his nature was sunny. Plutarch says he passed his whole life jesting and laughing. I believe he joked here, since Hipparchia gave him a son, and two daughters who grew up and married philosophers.

The brother of Hipparchia, Metrocles, became a disciple of Crates in the following manner: while he was rehearsing a public speech, he accidentally farted and, in despair at this breach of good manners, shut himself in the house intending to starve to death. Crates, known as the "Door-Opener" because he entered anywhere he pleased to admonish and harangue those within and so free their minds of evil, visited him but argued in vain. Finally Crates himself let fly a fart, thus restoring Metrocles to self-respect, who concluded he had committed no crime and thankfully became a lifelong disciple.

Democritus, finding the condition of man absurd and ridiculous, laughed. Heraclitus, finding man's condition to be exactly the same, wept.

> But Hudibras, who scorned to stoop
> To fortune, or be said to droop,
> Cheered up himself with ends of verse
> And sayings of philosophers.

Man on a Horse

Sir Hudibras wore but one spur,
Believing were he to bestir
By goad or prick one side of his horse
The other side must join, perforce,
Its partner in a jog or trot.

He held this theory. I do not,
But, honoring as I do those talents
Of equilibrium and balance
Missing in Hudibras, make note
To keep an oar on each side of the boat.

N.C.
814
B   Bevington, Helen
      Beautiful lofty
    people.

N.C. 20 JAN 75   WP 9282
814
B   Bevington, Helen
      Beautiful lofty
    people.

10/25 18 OCT 74   WP 22821
12/6 29 NOV 74   WP 16062
    17 FEB 75   J 8267
    12 MAR 75   Kasey
    11 APR 75   WP 24200
    27 DEC 75   WP 18826
    26 JAN 76   WP 25001

9/74

Wilmington Public Library
Wilmington, NC 28401